I   h

T

M   ER

Sherry Shriner

ISBN: 0692728414

ISBN 13: 9780692728413

Table of Contents

Introduction

I don't even know how to begin. Since writing my first two books Bible Codes Revealed: The Coming UFO Invasion and Aliens On The Internet I've been busy with my weekly radio show on Blog Talk Radio and decoding and analyzing Bible Codes.

It has never gotten easy, or easier. The daily grind takes a toll. The attacks from everywhere and 'neverwhere' never end. When you're on everyone's hate list and assassination list there's only one thing you can do, put it in God's hands and keep the pedal to the metal.

I've always run full speed ahead and even a heart attack in October of 2015 hasn't slowed me down much. I knew it was just the haters. One of their useless and constant attacks against me to silence me and shut me up once and for all. And to stop my war against them.

Who is 'them'? Lucifer's terrestrial offspring...his reptile people on, above, and below the earth. Through organizations such as the Illuminati he controls almost every government and military on earth.

His reptile faction, known as the lizards, dominate earth with their superior technology, advanced mind control and MK Ultra programs, and human bodily possession known as soul scalping.

I have been exposing how he works for over 15 years now, although I've been familiar with him my entire life. When I was younger I just didn't know enough to be able to put it all together. And when I finally did, it would become a constant battle against him and his forces. One that is very real even now that I fight against daily.

This book hasn't been professionally edited. I decided to just keep it raw, and real. My conversations with the devil, with Lucifer himself, stand on their own as is. I never changed or edited anything he said or I said. I just wanted to keep it real. So forgive all the grammatical errors, the broadcast style writing I've always been accustomed to, the commas that should be or shouldn't be and all the other grammatical mistakes I know I've made. It just is what it is. Real.

I guess I should introduce myself to those of you who aren't familiar with who I am or my work. Although being black listed from radio and TV there are millions around the world very familiar with who I am. I have a weekly Monday night radio show on the internet via Blog Talk Radio called Sherry Talk Radio. I run the popular websites www.TheWatcherFiles.com and www.SherryShriner.com. And I started an Orgone War back in 2004 that is putting balance back in our atmosphere, crashing UFOs, obliterating alien Star Ships and planets, and creating literal havoc on Lucifer that you can read more about at www.OrgoneBlasters.com

During my interviews with Lucifer you will hear him refer to the Orgone, my Orgone. Because it destroys him, it's very real. Not everyone who makes or sells Orgone is making or selling effective Orgone. It is my particular brand of Orgone that kills, destroys, and harms aliens and their habitations. And that's why it makes him so angry.

I am a born again believer in the Most High Yahuah and His Son Yahushua ben David (whom the churches call Jesus). I prefer to call them by their real names or Yah for short, which means "God" in Hebrew.

I have been a Christian my entire life and as you will hear from Lucifer himself, targeted for death my entire life as well...by him directly.

There are many eye-opening truths revealed in this book that have never been spoken of and never been revealed before. As an Ambassador, Messenger and Prophetess of the Most High I have sought Him for the truth in all things my entire life and always encourage others to do the same. Lucifer has worked tirelessly to suppress the truth, limit it, mask it and hide it. And that's why Father has stood me up to reveal it.

In this book I reveal what the Elect are, what it was really like during Lucifer's rebellion and war against Heaven, what really happened in the Garden of Eden, what's really going on at the Vatican today, and Lucifer's plans for the future.

All I can do is give you the truth. What you do with it is up to you.

Chapter One

Angels In The Flesh

This is abbreviated excerpts of a chapter from my previous book "Aliens On The Internet" that I published in 2008. The significance of the information in this chapter is imperative for people to understand so they can learn and realize the mechanics of how both heaven and hell operate here on earth.

♦ ♦ ♦

The battle of good and evil. It never stops. A perpetual war from the time you were born. Nevermind the war has gone on for thousands of years behind the scenes in a realm we cannot see. It has always been a war and it is always been a war for your soul, and yet few people understand the depths of it, fewer realize their own role in it.

A concept once understood, it has been buried during the church age. Knowledge once taken for granted by our Hebrew forefathers, now vehemently protested against by the church age false prophets put in place and influenced to keep the people of the Lord dumbed down and clueless.

What is it they don't want you to know?

Have we ever really grasped the concept of the spiritual realm that operates around us? And who we are?

Let's start at the basics.

Spirits are not only souls, but a name for Angels: For example,

Zec 6:5 And the angel answered and said unto me, These are the four spirits of the heavens, which go forth from standing before the Lord of all the earth. (we know them through the book of Enoch as Gabriel, Michael, Uriel, and Raphael)

Rev 1:4 John to the seven churches which are in Asia: Grace be unto you, and peace, from him which is, and which was, and which is to come; and from the seven Spirits which are before his throne;

Rev 3:1 And unto the angel of the church in Sardis write; These things saith he that hath the seven Spirits of God, and the seven stars; I know thy works, that thou hast a name that thou livest, and art dead.

Rev 4:5 And out of the throne proceeded lightnings and thunderings and voices: and there were seven lamps of fire burning before the throne, which are the seven Spirits of God.

Rev 5:6 And I beheld, and, lo, in the midst of the throne and of the four beasts, and in the midst of the elders, stood a Lamb as it had been slain, having seven horns and seven eyes, which are the seven Spirits of God sent forth into all the earth.

These Spirits are Angels.

Lucifer also has his own spirits, "For they are the spirits of devils, working miracles, which go forth unto the kings of the earth and of the whole world, to gather them to the battle of that great day of God Almighty" Rev 16:14. These are literal people who work with and for him.

And we were admonished by the Apostle John, "Beloved, believe not every spirit, but try the spirits whether they are of God: because many false prophets are gone out into the world" I John 4:1.

This is something the Lord showed me recently when I was doing a word search on the term Spirits. It all started unraveling before my eyes as He opened my eyes to reveal more of this truth to me. He has been showing me this truth over the past several months through various ways but when it started jumping out at me again during the study on Spirits in the Scriptures recently I knew it was time to reveal it.

The Bible mentions various types of spirits: familiar spirits, unclean spirits (Matt. 10:1), evil spirits (Matt. 8:16), seducing spirits (I Tim. 4:1), angels spirits (Heb.1:7), and ministering spirits. Devils are also referred to as spirits (Matt. 8:16) and people are referred to as spirits: "By which also he went and preached unto the spirits in prison" 1 Peter 3:19.

Yahweh or Yahuah (the way I prefer to spell His Name as it sounds and is pronounced) is the Father of all spirits, the creator:

> Num 16:22 And they fell upon their faces, and said, O God, the God of the spirits of all flesh,
> Num 27:16 Let the LORD, the God of the spirits of all flesh,
> Hbr 12:9 Furthermore we have had fathers of our flesh which corrected [us], and we gave [them] reverence: shall we not much rather be in subjection unto the Father of spirits, and live?

A spirit is a human soul that has left the body. It also is another name for angels. Angels don't have flesh bodies. However they can appear in human form when necessary and still be spirits. When Jesus arose from the dead He was a Spirit, yet he mingled with the apostles and others for 40 days before He ascended into heaven. He had a body that looked human, it just wasn't one made of flesh. Angels have appeared to humans such as Abraham, Lot, and the Scriptures say we can entertain angels and be unaware of it. Although they look human, can eat and drink like humans, they are not human bodies and they have supernatural capabilities.

It is Yahuah who created and creates spirits. When angels rebel against Him they become fallen angels and lose their first estate which is called heaven. Heaven is where the angels reside or have access to. It is their home. When they rebel against the Most High they are kicked out and must make their home somewhere else until they are judged for their rebellion. Some are judged right away, others are allowed to wait until the end of the age for their judgment.

As humans, we have souls which are our spirits, they are one in the same, they never die, however they live in a flesh body that does. The body will die but the spirit or soul will live on forever. A human is not immortal, but a spirit is.

According to Strong's dictionary a soul is a living, breathing being with life in the blood. It is a person himself or herself, the inner being of that person, their mind, emotions, it is what makes you, you. It is also your spirit. Strong says a spirit is the power by which the human being feels, thinks, decides, the vital principal by which the body is animated, the soul. The spirit and the soul are the same thing. Put inside of flesh, they become what we call a human, what the Lord refers to as mankind.

The Lord never refers to His creation as humans, but mankind. Man made in His kind of image. Mankind. Human is a pagan term for the sun god. Therefore mankind are spirits and angels placed in flesh or what most call human bodies.

What most people don't realize is that there are good spirits and angels of God put in flesh bodies and there are bad spirits and angels of Lucifer placed in flesh bodies.

Have we all existed before as spirits or angels and then placed into a fleshly body? Or are we a new creation put in a flesh body? I think either one can happen.

Those born from above, are Yahuah's.

Which means, not all are born from above.

Only those with His Spirit can be redeemed, those born from above.

> John 3:3 Jesus answered and said unto him, Verily, verily, I say unto thee, Except a man be born again, he cannot see the kingdom of God.
> John 3:7 Marvel not that I said unto thee, Ye must be born again.

In the Greek this should have been translated "born from above" and not "born again." In the Strong's the term born again means from above, from a higher place, of things which come from heaven or God, from the first, from the beginning, from the very first, and anew, over again. In other words, it should read, "except a man be born from above, he cannot see the kingdom of God" and "ye must be born from above."

The Apostle Peter says, "Being born again, not of corruptible seed, but of incorruptible, by the word of God, which liveth and abideth for ever" I Peter 1:23. Those from Yahuah and redeemed in Him are those that are born from above by incorruptible seed.

Which means, there are those walking among us today, who cannot be redeemed, because they were sent here by Lucifer himself and of corruptible seed. In other words, they are of his lineage or they are one of his spirits (angels) placed in a human body to do his will.

You have to remember Lucifer mimics and copies everything Yahuah does and Yahuah allows it to serve His own purposes.

It explains how some people can be inherently wicked and evil and think nothing of it. They do not have a consciousness of the Most High or of the things of heaven, or of good things. Evil and wickedness is what rules them. They are from the underworld to begin with. They are from their father, the devil. Some are sent by Lucifer directly for a specific purpose or reason. In the Hebrew Masoretic text the name of Saul itself means "underworld, borrowed." There are many sent by him who aren't named the name of Saul directly, but it is interesting that the one dominant Saul of our time is Saul of Tarsus who changed his name to Paul to hide his identity.

This whole understanding of Spirits clears up and confirms even more what people believe as my most controversial teachings, the Serpent seedline offspring and the Satanic infiltration of Saul-Paul-Satan into the church. I love how the Lord works, He always brings things back into a circle. A piece here, a piece there, then back again with more pieces to fit into the puzzle.

In my article entitled "The Serpent Seedline:Edomite Jews and the Sons of Cain" I talked about the two different groups of people throughout the Bible and our past, present, and future. Those who are elected to grace while the other is elected for wrath and destruction. These are two specific groups with two specific elections and only they can hold these elections, no one else is like them.

Are all those born into a specific family seedline corruptible or incorruptible? No. Although it may sound like it means just that, it does not mean that all. That would be like saying all those born into a cursed seedline are doomed for hell and all those born into Yahuah's chosen seedline are awarded heaven.

There are three major aspects that come into play at all times in regarding all things. The choices Yahuah makes, the choices Lucifer makes, and the individual choices we make.

Esau was born of a good seedline but he chose to go the way of the wicked. Just as those born of cursed seedlines can choose to go the way of the righteous. Do we choose or are we chosen ahead of time to do exactly what we do? Yahuah knows the end from the beginning and He knows those who are His and those who are not because He knows exactly what is going to happen. And He places His chosen vessels of honor anywhere He wants to, good or bad seedline. And Lucifer will do the same thing, except his vessels are of dishonor.

In other words, Yahuah can and does places chosen vessels of honor throughout the offspring of His children and of Lucifer's. And Lucifer does the same thing.

We have the children of Israel, the children of Cain, and the Gentile nations who are judged in how they treat the children of Israel. Can they be redeemed? Yes if they adopt Yahushua as their Savior and accept and receive His salvation. If they are born from above, they are one of His spirits to begin with. Remember His Spirits are everywhere, placed in all nations, but those of His must choose Him of their own free will. Being a spirit from above doesn't ensure salvation, you must choose Him.

What I have been led to believe based on Scripture is that there are three major seedlines of people in this world today. Those directly of Yah, those directly of Satan, and gentiles, the other nations inbred and created from hybrid offspring from the other two lines and carried out throughout the centuries. There are many nations of people considered as Gentiles back in the earlier days, those who were not Israelite, and not all of those lines were purposeful offspring from Lucifer either. They are hybrid races, mixtures from both lines and whose continuity just grew and spread out throughout the ages. It is these nations who are judged at the end of the tribulation period in how they treated Israel...those who accepted Yahushua as Savior.

Most people don't realize that we, America, most of Europe, Australia, and Canada are Israel. We didn't replace Israel, we ARE Israel. There were 14 tribes spread out among the earth. The Jews in rule in Israel today are not real Jews, refer to Rev. 2:9 and 3:9. They are Turks, known as Khazarians or Khazars posing as Jews and even Orthodox Jews.

On this earth, there is a perpetual war between the children of Father, the Most High, and the children of Lucifer. Lucifer can corrupt Yahuah's people and Yahuah can call out those He placed in Lucifer's offspring leading them to salvation.

Lucifer can place his spirit in people, just as Yahuah does. We saw what happened to Judas who betrayed Jesus (Yahushua) born of corruptible seed (did not I call 12 of you and one of you is a devil?") and we've been having to deal with Saul, born of corruptible seed, and how he has infiltrated and destroyed the churches and Christianity with false doctrines as a servant from Satan.

There are many brought to this earth for specific reasons. To fulfill certain roles and assignments, both for Yahuah and Lucifer.

Yahuah told the Prophet Jeremiah He knew him before He was born. Because He sent Jeremiah here with a specific role to fulfill. In fact many of His people were chosen ahead of time to come here when they did to fulfill a specific purpose. They were begotten from above and then sent here on earth to live in flesh bodies.

Those who choose to serve Satan do so because he is their father. The Antichrist and False Prophet will be those sent of him to do his will on earth. They are borrowed from the underworld and put here in human flesh to fulfill these roles.

Once you realize how it is, then some of you can stop thinking of how mean the Lord is for causing the False Prophet and Antichrist to be born just to burn in the lake of fire later. They were of Satan to begin with and unredeemable. When they were born his spirit was placed inside them, not Yahuah's. And these people don't want redeemed, they hate the Most High as much as their father the devil does. Do not pity these haters of Yahuah, rather pray for their judgment! Lucifer's spirits placed in these people are the same angels who rebelled against the Most High during Lucifer's rebellion in the previous civilization now coming back to earth to help him do it again!

The church is soft on evil. They may as well lay a pillow out and welcome mat for those who do evil. Why? Because they misinterpret Scriptures.

Yahushua called Satan's seed fools and vipers, to be cast into the lake of fire. He didn't mince words with them or feign love toward them. He knew what and who they were. And He made a distinction between Satan's seed and those who were redeemable, even with the Gentiles. He offered His salvation to the Gentiles, He will not cast aside anyone who seeks Him. But He knows the born from below serpent seeds will never seek His redemption and it was those He spoke against openly during His ministry here.

Born from below. Angels who rebelled against the Most High in the past and re-born through human flesh to serve Lucifer's purposes again, this time as humans.

Born from above. Angels who love the Most High and are sent down here to be born as humans to serve His purposes and fulfill a calling for Him as humans. Yes, there are people, begotten from the beginning as angels to fulfill certain roles on earth as humans. They are sent down here on purpose to fulfill a certain role and when they die(d) they went or go back up to be with Him.

This is a truth that is part of the ancient wisdom and mysteries that mankind once knew. Yahuah told me there are many things in the Scriptures that we have been blinded to.

Angels in human flesh. Good and bad angels with roles to play in these last days. It is a war between God and Satan, between heaven and hell.

Yahuah is revealing to some of His people their former names and even ranks in heaven. So is Lucifer. He is gathering his own people together for the final onslaught against Yahuah chosen. So this information is going to start coming out and just because the churches ignore it doesn't mean it is not true, it means they are doing their usual job of suppressing the truth. The Whores of Babylon. Lucifer doesn't want Yahuah people to seek Him to know if they are an angel in flesh with a specific calling and purpose. He wants them to stay ignorant of who and what they are so they don't fulfill it.

Seek the Lord, the Most High for the truth, to confirm or reject what I am saying Himself. Don't allow Lucifer to keep you in division, anger, and bickering with your brethren just so you stay in the dark. Yahuah has revealed this truth to me and has many more things to reveal to me if there is time. If I have time. Be diligent and seek Him in all things and ask Him every day to reveal the truth to you in all things.

The war is on. Many of Satan's know who they are. Many of Yahuah's know who they are. Yahuah's army seeks to build and edify Him, to preach and teach His truth and prepare His people for what is ahead. They are good shepherds and take care of His flock and serve Him. Satan seeks to destroy Yahuah's people, to fleece them and hold them in bondage to false doctrines, guile and witchcraft and idolatry.

Test the spirits-angels in human flesh - whether they be of God. Seek HIM. He who denies Jesus Christ, Yahushua came in the flesh (and died on the cross for the redemption of mankind) is an Antichrist.

"He that hath hath an ear let him hear what the Spirit saith unto the churches; To him that overcometh will I give to eat of the hidden manna and will give him a white stone and in the stone a new name written, which no man knoweth saving he that receiveth it" Rev. 2:17.

For those who hold steadfast to the faith, even unto death, they will be given a new name in heaven. In the Strong's a name can signify one's rank and authority, it can also describe their works and interests.

This is your new name as a heavenly being. The former things of earth over time will be forgotten.

All beings are created with free will. Even angels can use their free will to abandon heaven and Yahuah. He holds no one a prisoner.

...in fact...

Some of these very angels, who led the rebellion against Lucifer (in the past), begged the Most High to be sent here on earth to be born in bodies of flesh to do it once again in the last days. These are the ones, born from above with a specific purpose and calling on their lives for the last days. The ones who stand up and openly war against Lucifer and his forces, they did it before and they are doing it again now as the prophetic time clock ticks for his arrival on earth and visible rule through the man we call the Antichrist.

Most of these angels sent from heaven to be born as humans are not born with the remembrance of having been in heaven. Over time the Most High will reveal it to them as they seek Him and walk with Him. They know they are here for a reason, they just don't know what. Most are targeted from the time they are born and Lucifer, knowing who they are, will try and kill and destroy them when they are children, or throughout their lives and these angel-people can't figure out why they are such targets and why things seem to happen to them unlike most people. They are here to fulfill Yahuah's purposes in the last days.

Yahuah told me I begged Him to let me come down here for the last days. That I made a promise and oath to Him that if He let me come down here I would become one of Lucifer's biggest enemies. He has told me my mission has been accomplished.

I have spent my entire life at odds and at war against the evil realm of the supernatural. Against Lucifer. He sent his generals to kill me when I was a child and even stalked me himself on many occasions, watching me grow up.

Today I have over 10 websites exposing his plans, strategies, tactics and general mayhem as he uses governments, religion and his own forces to infiltrate and destroy our planet.

I run discussion lists and a weekly radio program to inform and teach Yahweh's people about the past, present and future. I have published two books incorporating the articles on my websites to make it easier to read all at once, and have several others on the back burner simply because if I want to publish them my way I have to publish them myself and I don't have the funds to publish them. I have started and created a network of Yahuah's people to make and plant a weapon we call orgone that will and is protecting them from the attacks of our government and Lucifer's forces we call aliens.

I have spent my life in service to the Most High in one way or another while others spend theirs criticizing and hating me. Serving the Most High means having to put up and with and tolerating those who claim they love Him yet don't know Him at all. He can't lead them out of their errors because they want to stay in them. They put their trust and faith in man and head knowledge never learning how to seek Him and be filled with heart knowledge of the Most High. An outcast, a soldier in the wilderness, there are many of us like this.

In these last days Yahuah is leading these people together. In these last days, Lucifer's own toy, the internet, has become an instrumental source in those begotten by Yahuah and sent here for the last days to find each other. The Lord is raising His people up to do battle against the evil and wickedness of the New World Order and Lucifer's other pet projects to destroy and enslave the souls of mankind.

As those begotten for these last days come to the knowledge of who they are, there is no stopping them. They will stand and fight fearlessly against Lucifer under the protection of the Most High or support those who do. And when their missions are completed, their protection will be lifted, and they will leave earth and go back home.

I once heard that the Lord sent His best for last. If so, what are you doing for Him today and where are you in the mix? Are you helping in keeping His people united and focused on the Most High and preparing them for these last days or fighting against those who are because they are not a part of your denomination or group? Or are you so far gone in the wants and cares of this world that you simply don't care about the things that mean the most to the Most High? If you love this world and the things in it then you are of this world. Those of Yahuah seek Him and the things from above. Lucifer uses division and hatred among Yahuah's people to keep them divided and of no threat to him.

If you are one of the Lord's and you know you are, stand alone if you have to. Just stand up and get busy with what He leads you to do. Time is short.

Chapter Two

The Beginning: Shazurazy

Growing Up In Heaven

As one of these angels in the flesh and from the past, I already have a long history with Hallayel, who became known as Lucifer and Satan. He was my brother. And all of heaven disowned him and refused to call him by his angel name after he rebelled against it...which is why he is now called Lucifer.

It is these "Angels in the Flesh" who in the Bible are called the Elect, the Firstborn, the First Fruits...those terms have nothing to do with Christians and a rapture, but Father's Firstborn, those who were angels in heaven and then sent to earth to be born as humans to fulfill roles on earth...just as Yahushua, Jeremiah, John the Baptist, and others had been.

In Biblical terms the Elect and the Bride are two different groups of people.

I decided to write this book and incorporate all the information I have learned the past 8 years from talking to the Father and the many, many hours of even talking to Lucifer and Lillith themselves in regards to the information I have been gathering and posting online and revealing on my radio show.

How is it even possible for me to talk to Lucifer? Because Lucifer has been detained in a lower realm of heaven since March, 2016. And it's because of this detainment that Father has made it possible for me to talk to Lucifer, which ultimately became the series of interviews for this book.

In February, 2016 Lillith spear headed a global assassination attack against me using both their sisterhood and brotherhood's to unite and come against me via black magic circles and chanting to cause me to have a fatal heart attack (their earlier attempt in October, 2015 had failed to kill me). When I appealed to Father and told Him I would die if they didn't stop their chanting against me He sent the archangel Michael to capture and detain Lillith. Since then they have held her captive in a lower realm of heaven.

The next month in March Lucifer would instigate a fight against me with many of his forces from space. He used this feigned attack as a distraction to sneak away and go to heaven and attempt to free Lillith from her imprisonment. He was captured by an Archangel and put into captivity and detained with her instead. He has been there with her since.

During this time I had thought it would be interesting to actually ask the horses themselves about their perspectives of the past...the era of the flood, the Garden of Eden, Lucifer's rebellion against Heaven, and whatever else came to mind. Father not only allowed it but mediated and accommodated it as well.

When you have Satan or Lillith in any realm in heaven and have them agree to be interviewed and answer questions they're not going to sit and lie, not with Father being there...so it's been an interesting venture... and one I was enjoying until it got to the obvious point when I would have to talk about myself and reveal who I am because I hate that stuff...I hate talking about myself...especially to a world of haters, uninformed, clueless or just unbelieving mockers. But unless you know who I was in the past then the following interviews wouldn't make any sense because Lucifer and I know each other very well...and it comes across clearly that we had a past with each other and now share the same space and time on earth together. As I revealed earlier Lucifer was my brother....because I, Sherry Shriner, am an angel in the flesh, an angel from the past, a queen even, known as Queen Shazurazy in heaven.

On earth I'm just a humble grandmother, mother, and servant of the Most High who figured out a way (with some help) to kick Lucifer's butt above, on, and below the earth and so I started a ministry and an Orgone War and have spent almost two decades trying to eliminate his reptiles and terrestrial beings off our planet.

So that's me in a nutshell and you'll learn more from the interviews. But first Father wants me to tell you what I remember about Heaven, which isn't much, but the memories I do have are priceless to me.

◆ ◆ ◆

My earliest memories are of sitting on the Father's lap as a baby angel. His throne was so huge. I would describe it at least 100 feet high and at least 50 feet wide. Ok maybe about 10 feet high and 5 feet wide but when it sits on a platform it seems so much bigger. My sister and I would play in the throne room just to be with dad. We loved Him and He was always so funny, and warm, and loving. I was the youngest of 12 girls and 2 boys. All created directly by the Father as His own children with His Spirit and particular attributes directly in us. I would say DNA but that's human terminology and we were spiritual beings of another dimension and realm.

I was probably about 2 feet high at the time and learning how to fly with wings was fun. I remember sitting on his lap and then crawling up to the top of his chair, throne, and him muttering "oh my" and I would get Rashayel to climb up there with me and then we'd jump off the top of the throne and flitter to the ground. It was a good 20 feet or higher. We would laugh and giggle and do it over and over until dad would say "ok girls, let's do something else!" But he always let us have our fun for a while, he was patient, kind, he'd giggle and act like a typical dad letting his kids have some fun, knowing we were safe with Him. We knew that some day we would grow up to be tall, commanding angels, princesses, queens, daughters of the Most High but until then we were just going to have some fun!

It's the memories of the past that Father would give me, that would keep me going when the battles here on earth would get tiring, overbearing, and I would just burn out with a desire to just walk away from all of it.

He would give me memories to revitalize, strengthen, help me to remember who I was, where I came from, and typically just make me laugh and miss home.

I remember my sisters. Rashayel was the one directly above me in numbers. She was #13 and I was #14. Father had 14 kids. Hadassah was the oldest. And other than Rashayel, I remember her the most. If memories have anything to say about it, then I was probably the closest to Rashayel, Hadassah, Ella, Branz, Yasha, and Hallayel because those are the ones I remember the most. Although I loved them all very much. I can remember all of us girls piled up in this one room in the palace in what could probably be described as lounge chairs and couches. Talking and gabbing, and a couple of them would be cutting and sewing, and creating new gowns, robes, whatever our attire was. Two of the sisters were really into fashion and would work with seamstresses to create new clothes for us all. I called them the Designers. Clothes were just a small part of what they would actually do. They would design planets, landscapes, whatever was needed, they would design it. They were engineers, architects, designers.

What makes me laugh today is to hear the term 'flower girls' because some of my fondest memories are hanging out with the two sisters who would journey to far away places just to find the perfect flowers for the palace. And that's what me and Rashayel always referred to them as, the flower girls. We would go with them on some of their trips and journeys just to play with whatever we could find to play with. We didn't have much on our minds at the time, just always looking to have some fun. A hill or mountain would thrill us for hours. While the other girls would gather flowers with the entourage that was with us we would flitter to the top of the hills or mountains and free fall off of them and wait till the last possible seconds of hitting ground to pull out our wings to break our fall. We had so much fun doing that. It was one of our angel games.

We were far from typical. None of the other sisters or boys seemed to be anything like me or Rashayel. They were always content to be doing whatever they were doing. We preferred adventure, exploring, getting away from the palace and learning and doing new things. As we got older we demanded the Archangels teach us how to fly the air pods (otherwise they probably wouldn't have) And of course we found a way to make an angel game out of them. I would fly up underneath Rashayel's then rise up under one of the pod wings, flipping her over. I used to think that was so funny. Then she'd come right back at me and the battle was on. We would do that for hours, flying all over the place, flipping each other over. Then we'd go after the other angels with pods and flip them over. No one seem to mind. They would just laugh.

The queens were the closest to the Archangels who were also typically inside or around the palace in outside areas around it. The Archangels were always up for having some fun. They were great play-mates for me and Rashayel. I can remember working with Michael from the time I was practically created with gymnastics, tumbling, flying, warfare, sword fighting, all kinds of techniques and fighting...me and Rashayel had started very young with him as our teacher and trainer. We were all very close and that would come in handy for the day when me and Rashayel would turn in our angel games for swords, war and battle strategies.

I was about 6"2, as was Rashayel. That's not very tall for an angel. Angels are various sizes with a lot of them much taller perhaps. Probably the average or typical size that I can remember is about 6 - 7 foot. I was very blonde, bright blue eyes. I had long blonde hair, thin, considered very beautiful as were all the queens. Rashayel had long dark hair, blue eyes. She was the more analytical of the two of us. She was more of a thinker, level headed, more reserved. I was outgoing, crazy, didn't think of much except what to get into next and Rashayel would be right there beside me. We were always together. The girls were like twins, like we were created in pairs, because the girls were always with their counterpart, their twin, even if we weren't technically twins, it just seemed that way because of the pairings, if you saw one you'd see the other with them. That's just the way it was. I can't remember a time unless I was with Yasha or Hallayel that I wasn't with Rashayel. I don't remember where she would be when I was with one of the boys, but she was probably at the palace hanging out with the sisters in our lounge room.

I remember a few things about my brothers. I remember Yasha from the time I was practically created. Hallayel I remember as I got a little older. They were both my big brothers and I loved hanging out with them. When I was real little I can remember sitting on Yasha's lap and he would hold me and hug me and make me laugh. We would talk and sing and he would teach me new songs. We would take walks through pastures filled with beautiful flowers and he would hold my hand and we would walk, skip, run, and laugh. He was the best big brother.

Hallayel was awesome to. He was charming, smart, and he loved music. He would always teach me how to play musical instruments and let me watch him command orchestras, or choirs, or watch him create and compose music. He could play anything and he liked all the different types of music we had up there. He was always busy with the music but he always had time for me when I'd come around. He'd ask me if I was practicing my instruments or we'd go run and play in one of the fields that surrounded the palace.

He would take me for walks or take me somewhere and show me something new. He always had something to say, something interesting to talk about, he was full of excitement, energy, fun, adventure, and he would showcase it in his music, he would create master pieces, everyone revered his talent. Angels would come from everywhere to listen to him sing, play, perform, lead, direct. He did it all...he could have been a one man orchestra, one man band. As I got older if I wanted to see him I would have to go find him because he was always some place else, working on his music, giving concerts, or getting involved with running administration and angelic affairs. He was just generally away a lot of the time. And I started to see him less and less.

I remember as I was getting older, probably what we consider as teenage years here, that Hallayel began to teach me how to play what we would call a guitar. It was a bit different in heaven. In heaven you didn't need to plug it in to electricity, as there was no need for it there. It would just play loud the way it was. Something like an acoustic guitar but less strings and a lot louder. And it actually sounded a lot more awesome than guitars here on earth. And he had been spending a lot of time to teach me how to play it. I got very good at it...and together we could definitely "jam the guitar" so to say. In our own angel way. I loved ballads and long instrumental solos. It was my favorite instrument.

People in general don't think of heaven as having anything more than harps and church choir type music but that isn't true. There was all different types of music in heaven. The biggest difference would be the lyrics and heavier demonic beats that music on earth has.

I can remember times when Yasha would come into the Lounge Room to hang out with his sisters. We all loved those times. We'd love to see him and we would all gab, and joke and goof around. As I try to remember back, I don't remember any times that Hallayel ever came into the Lounge. For some reason he never did. And I don't remember him and Rashayel ever being together either. I know I certainly don't remember everything and perhaps a lot of things are blocked, but it seems odd to me that there's just some things I can't remember at all and that in particular is Hallayel's relationship with the others, or lack of it.

When I asked Father about it, He told me that Hallayel, as brilliant as he was, was always very insecure. And the reason I was the one that was closest to him was because I would always run after him as a child to be with him. Where the others were more reserved and stayed around the Palace or did what it was they were supposed to be doing, I was running all over the place and hanging out with everyone. I built relationships with everyone because I loved everyone. I didn't know a stranger, if I didn't know an angel I'd make them my friend. That's just the kind of person or angel I was. I was very outgoing and very friendly. And that's why I got along so good with Hallayel. I was his favorite sister because I was really the only one he was close to. I don't know why he never built relationships with the others. I thought maybe he had and I just couldn't remember but Father told me that no, Hallayel never had, that he was never close to the others. I just find that so odd.

I think people have the idea that all angels know each other. That's not true. There are billions of them and they are spread out everywhere. There wasn't just one place or planet for them. There were many.

The few memories I have here on earth are the ones that suit Father's purposes for the here and now. Because remembering the past would bridge the present and perhaps explain why a brother and sister that were once so close, could over time, become rivals, even arch enemies, and fight against each other for over a million years culminating with an epic war on earth that only the Father Himself could finish.

This is one of the greatest stories never told. And I'm going to try to tell it the best I can.

Heaven

The Sun was known as the Yahuan Star Gate and it was the Yahuan's Helio Star System - what we know as Heaven.

Heaven itself is its own galaxy within our universe. I can remember about 24 other universes existing around us somewhere but I've never been to any of them that I know of. I don't even know anything about them and there are perhaps, probably a lot more than just 24. I just remember that number for some reason. And if I ever was at others, I simply don't remember.

Heaven is a galaxy within a universe. Very much like Earth is today, a planet within the Milky Way Galaxy. The name Heaven is a concept from people themselves. Once mankind was created on a re-created Earth it was the people that would refer to it as Heaven because it would encompass the area above them, their atmosphere, their space, ultimately the space above space, what would be considered Heaven. To us it was just home. I don't remember a particular name for it, or the name of our galaxy, or universe, in the scheme of things. It was just home.

For simplicity and the sake of the readers of this book who couldn't imagine it being called anything else, I'll just refer to it as heaven.

Heaven was made up of, and still is, multiple planets. There are cities on all of them and with the huge landscapes the beauty is simply breathtaking. You don't realize just how beautiful it all is until you're not there anymore and all you have are vague memories of a time that once was, and a time you're literally dying to return to. After all, anyone born on earth is born to eventually die. You just have no idea how long or short your time on earth will be. And to return to Heaven or to get to heaven upon death, you have to qualify. I'll talk about qualifications later. For now I just want to describe Heaven itself.

When I was growing up there were 14 planets of Heaven. Earth was the last planet created and I was destined to become the ruler over it. Back then it was known as Shan. And I, Queen Shazurazy would become the ruler over Shan. Each of Father's direct children would rule over one of the planets. Yasha would rule over what we know as Venus. Because Venus was the closest to the Sun and the time would come when Yasha would sit at Father's right hand. Rashayel ruled over what was known as Urantia, now a destroyed planet called Uranus. Well, all of the planets were destroyed, mostly into oblivion. Hallayel's planet was called Tiamet and it was completely blown up into smithereens during the War. Shan was destroyed by me, practically by myself in my anger against it. Just as Rashayel would destroy hers. And together we would lead the destruction of all the others.

The Palace was in an area all itself. I guess you could call it a planet. The palace was a huge area with many fields and country sides surrounding all sides of it. Everything was made of some type of brilliant white marble or stone. It was almost as if it was so white it glowed. All of the buildings in heaven, either on the Palace planet or any of the others were made with this white stone or gem stone, or marble, I simply don't remember what it was.

Gemstones were also a big part of design and architecture of cities, buildings, and landscapes. As were the garments we would wear. Robes, colors, sashes, cords, swords for the warriors, everything was precise and significant in meaning. There were ranks, classifications, and levels of angels. Some angels would have horses and command hosts of warriors on horses that could walk, run, and even fly in and out of portals. Where others would have air pods suited to fly out of heaven's realm and into others and we didn't need fuel for them. The majority of angels would stay within the areas of heaven itself and had their own angelican air pods to use to travel from one planet or "house" to another. We didn't refer to them as planets. They were called Houses.

There was no pollution. We didn't need telephones as we could talk to each other no matter where we were via an inner spirit communication, or what most refer to as telepathy. There is no death in heaven, or darkness, or night time, or time itself. I can't even begin to equate how long a million years in heaven would be in earth's time.

In the Bible it quotes on earth in regards to creation that a thousand years is as a day. Perhaps a million years in Heaven is as a thousand years on Earth. I kind of get the feeling that that's probably correct. As I sit here and muse over time itself since heaven doesn't operate in Earth's linear time, Father tells me the parallel or correlation itself is very accurate. A Million years in heaven's time, would correlate to a Thousand years on Earth. Good, that's settled, for whatever reason. I guess it's just interesting to know.

There were angel communities everywhere. And every House (planet) had it's own distinct nature to it and types of communities.

The Palace, I don't know what else to call it so on Earth I've referred to it as the Royal Planet or RP, there were angel communities of those who worked at or served in the Palace in some way.

Angel marriages were allowed if they were ordained by Father Himself. If they were ordained by Him they would last forever. There were no divorces, ever, that I can remember. And angels had children. Some groups of angels weren't capable of having them where other classifications and types of angels could. There were different types of angels, what we would call races, or nations. Only it didn't have anything to do with skin color, all angels were white. But some were made differently than others. Some classifications could procreate where other classifications couldn't. It wasn't a big deal in Heaven. Angels weren't being created to grow up and raise families. It wasn't like that at all. But within the classifications of angels that could, it would happen. After earth was created many of the angels would adopt the children and babies that had died on Earth and would raise them as their own.

The churches misconstrue one passage of Scripture that says angels don't' procreate to generalize all of them and that isn't true. There is much about Heaven that has never been revealed or accurately spoke about. It doesn't mean what's been said before is wrong, it just means they're limited in knowledge and only going by what they know. We've all been extremely limited in knowledge and even I deal with memory blocks from Father Himself. That's just the way it is. It isn't right or wrong, it just is.

I can remember a lake in one of the angel communities not far from the Palace. Rashayel and I would go over and think of games to play, watch others, and just splash water all day. There were fountains in the lake we would fly and spin around, there were bridges over it we could jump off of. There was an air pod parking garage we would jump off the roof into the water. Not to far away were streets and rows of mansions with big beautiful homes where top ranking angels would live who served the Palace directly. Everyone who lived on the Royal Planet could just fly to the Palace themselves. No pods or horses were needed to get there unless you wanted one. Queens had horse led carriages they would use to get around in, and the horses could fly. It was awesome. I'm sure that's where Hallayel got the idea for Santa and his flying reindeer. He's not very original.

We had this one game called bat ball, or wing ball. It was very much like what we have volleyball here. Only we would throw the ball up in the air and use our wings to hit it. And the court itself was like the size of a soccer field because when we hit it with our wings the ball could fly a great distance.

One time when we had gotten older me and Rashayel were at the Palace standing on a hill beside the Palace and down below us were a bunch of Archangels doing various things, gabbing, goofing around, so me and Rashayel started winging balls at them, just pelting them, and as they were yelling and running and trying to wing balls back at us while the other sisters joined in. It was war. You couldn't see Him, but you could hear Father's laughter.

The best of the best could be found on the Royal Planet. The best of music, art, food, wine, literature, warriors, and gladiators. Supreme Councils were located in areas of various cities that governed over the Councils of the various Houses. The members of the local and regional House councils were elected by the angels who lived on that House. The members of the Supreme Councils were appointed by Father Himself because they were located on the Royal Planet. Every angel on the Royal Planet was appointed and assigned there by Father Himself. And they were given a mansion to live in for themselves or if they had a family then they would live there with them. Being appointed to the Royal Planet was the highest of honors.

Most people don't realize that heaven is a lot like Earth. After all, Hallayel, one of Father's own sons who rebelled against Him and left Heaven is the one who practically runs Earth and incorporates everything into it he experienced and lived in while he was in Heaven.

There are cafe's and coffee shop type places in Heaven. There are concerts and various venues you can go to for various things. There are video screens, where our TV flat screens were a mimic of where angels can view various things taking place. There is a planetary audio system in each House where announcements are made and can be heard simultaneously everywhere. You can hear music and angels singing. You can view the screens for announcements you may have missed. There isn't an 'angel Hollywood' nor movies, actors, actresses etc...but that's how Satan incorporated it into our world and used it to pervert, and influence people, just as he did music, wine, entertainment, and politics. Everything he incorporated he perverted and used for his own purposes to influence, degrade, and defile mankind.

One of my favorite venues in Heaven was to go and watch the gladiators. There were gladiator schools that taught interested angels how to fight. There were often competitions and tournaments where angels would seek to get promoted to higher levels and ranks as gladiators and warriors. Fighting wasn't a huge thing at the time although we had angelic posts located throughout the universe to guard against possible invading hostile visitors. If they somehow found a way to an outside area of our realm they would be chased out. If they made it inside they would have been instantly vaporized so the outer realm angelic posts were there to make sure they didn't cross the barrier or even find ways in to the inner realm which was Heaven. And to warn them off so they wouldn't get vaporized. No one just stumbles or invades, or comes into heaven, it's technically impossible. So basically the Warrior angels would just guard the outer areas. The same way they do today.

In heaven everything is free. But there are things you can trade and barter for that go above and beyond a basic necessity. You can always trade paintings or furniture for different paintings or furniture, or trade for something or whatever it is you see that you want. There's probably millions of brilliant artists in heaven and they always create things and give their paintings away for free. There's no money in heaven. You are either rewarded or appointed things, or you receive something you earned, but there is no market economy, Wall Street, greed, stealing, crime, and all the other things associated with money.

Angels govern their own communities and sign up for various services they work with. I wouldn't call them jobs, although that's a lot like what they are, you just don't get paid for it. Everyone volunteers their time for whatever service they are involved in or with. You can be a teacher, instructor, artist, painter, singer, run a cafe, coffee shop, make clothes, shoes, get elected to a council, you can be a record keeper, courier, warrior, gladiator, palace support personnel since there's a palace in every House. There's just a lot of different things you can do, no one sits around and does nothing. It's a lot like Earth, you spend part of the day at work and then relax the rest of the day. In Heaven since there's no night time to divide the day in half, it's a lot like shift work. You sign up for a particular shift and then go at the time that shift is on. I don't remember how the time is calculated there, it's just not like Earth's time.

Yahuah's Daughters and Sons And Their Attributes:

Hadasseh: Wisdom & Knowledge - Queen of Wisdom and Knowledge.
Elayzah: Wisdom & Understanding, temperance, patience, balance Queen of Understanding and Knowledge
Mikailez/Mickaylez (Mickey): Queen of Love, Honor, & Grace

Yalandah: Queen of Love, Joy, Peace,
Toriahn (Tory): Queen of Music, Composition & Harmony
Hallayel: King of Music, Praise, Harmony & Balance
Yasha: King of Perfection & Completion
Jaorgianne/Georgianne (JoJo): Queen of Perfection, Mediation, Temperance,
Ellashayzor (Ella): Artistic Design & Creativity (Engineer, Architect, Design, (all kinds all phases) Queen of Engineering and Artistic Design
Beranziana (Branz): Artistic Design & Creativity Queen of Engineering and Artistic Design Queen of Engineering & Technology
Nashahallah: Glory, Praise, & Worship - Queen of Worship
Lahandria: Glory, Praise, & Worship - Queen of Praise
Rashayel: Warrior, Judgment & Destroyer - Queen of Water
Shazurazy: Warrior, Judgment & Destroyer - Queen of Fire

Planets & Dwarfs which were all a part of the ancient Heavenly solar system under different or similar names and their rulers:

Earth - Shan - Shaz
Uranus - Urantia - Rashayel
Venus - Yasha
Tiamet - Hallayel
Mercury - Elayzah
Mars - Toriahn
Jupiter - Ellashayzor
Saturn - Beranziana
Neptune - Hadassah
Pluto - Lahandra
Eris - Georgianne
Haumea -Nashallah
MakeMake - Mickaylez
Ceres - Yahlanda

I know I have the first 9 correct but the last 5 I'm a bit iffy on. I could be wrong on those but whatever, there's many dwarfs in our solar system and all of the planets were moved around and knocked out of their original and normal orbits after the Judgment of the Houses began.

♦ ♦ ♦

What we have today is the remnant of what was once a very different looking type of solar system.

Recently I asked Lucifer why he was never close to anyone in the palace but me and he said, "I never felt a part of them...I always felt like an outsider, unappreciated, you were the one that made me feel wanted... you made me feel love, joy,.."

When I asked Father about growing up there He said:

You were an accomplished gladiator while you were growing up. Michael and the others had always worked with you and Rashayel in warfare and techniques of fighting. That's why on Shan you had it set up for gladiators and military training. You enjoyed all of that and were very involved with fighting in competitions and tournaments. No one could beat you....and since you were a queen, the archangels wouldn't fight you directly, even in fun, but Michael was always so proud of you. He would always cheer you on.

And so here it is. An unveiling of sorts. And perhaps it will give some people the answers they're looking for as to what would cause a queen from heaven to come down to earth to fight against her brother who had been excommunicated and kicked out of heaven.

Chapter Three

Shazurazy Part 2

The Rebellion & War

For some reason Lucifer was always insecure and never felt he got the attention from Father he deserved. Or craved from Him. I simply can't understand him. No one else felt ignored or that they didn't get attention from dad ..it was never an issue with anyone, we all loved dad and if we wanted to see Him we would go see Him..if He was busy with things we would see Him later but no one ever felt that that weren't loved by Him, ever. We all loved Him very much. To us He was and is 'dad' and during the interviews both Lucifer and I refer to Him as such).

Sherry - I don't know where Lucy's insecurity came from. Balance and Harmony were part of his attributes and yet he was completely unbalanced and unharmonic.

Sherry - insecurity feeds isolationism or even hatred. If it turns into hatred and anger that feeds into narcissism. Pride, boastfulness, are all traits of narcissism. An inflated, self-centered ego. If anyone would have known a problem was brewing within him it would have been Hadassah. And she would have gone straight to Father without necessarily going to anyone else about it or talking to anyone else.

Sherry - you could view it as he was a bad apple from the beginning. If there's a runt in every litter then he was it. No one else had insecurity issues and I certainly don't know how he got his.

Sherry - Lucifer had said, "I never felt a part of them...I always felt like an outsider, unappreciated, you were the one that made me feel wanted... you made me feel love, joy,.."

Lucifer - when I would go away for periods of time and come back they would be like "hey Halayel, how are you" etc....

Sherry - what did you expect a big party?

Lucifer - that would have been nice, something....

Sherry - you always felt under appreciated?

Lucifer - Yes.....

Sherry - Why didn't you ever have a relationship with Yasha?

Lucifer - he was awkward, he was always kissing up to Father and I would be out accomplishing and doing things and he would get all Father's attention.

Lucifer - there were 14, the girls all had one (planet) but I ruled over them because they were never around, they'd go running around or back to the palace with dad, I took care of things...I was more hands on with everyone, the girls were all beautiful and smart, but they let everyone run themselves, I was looking for better ways to do things, I was the one they liked to see show up, I made a lot of friends away from the palace and that's simply why I was never there.

Sherry - but you got influenced by a bad group of people...you let them influence you ....they pulled you away is what it is...

Lucifer, probably some of it, but I was getting tired of just being the under dog to Father all the time...I wanted to do things my way, I wanted to be the leader, not secondary to Father...I just rose above Him, it was time to just leave and take everything with me and away from Him.

Sherry - why couldn't you just serve Him like the rest of us did?

Lucifer - I was arrogant, I'll admit it, but I had fun...and once I made the move to break away it felt liberating...like I didn't have someone over my shoulder all the time...I couldn't stand that...

Sherry - yeah but He's still there...always...

Lucifer - yeah but I'm on my own...

Sherry - don't you think He's using you though? Using you to test the people?

Lucifer - laughs, if they loved Him they'd serve him. They love me. They don't care if they go to hell.

There seems to be a huge disconnect about Lucifer's rebellion from Heaven and the lack of information available on it. And it makes you wonder why, after all these years, Lucifer himself has been so silent about it.

Was he trying to hide who he was? Where he came from? I know that all the way up to 2014 no one even knew or realized he had a sister, let alone two here on earth. Who were busy in the background creating havoc against him.

But this is when Hallayel would become the Adversary against God. Satan means adversary and that name would be adopted for him by the time the KJV was written and passed down through the ages to the churches.

Lucifer means Light Bearer and I'm not sure when he was appointed that name, or who appointed it. It was just another name that was attributed to him.

Most of those around him today and those in the occultic groups refer to him as Luce, or Lucifer. While those in the churches for the most part refer to him as Satan, or the devil.

No one has ever referred to him by his original angelic name but me. When I wrote an article years ago referencing his real name and referred to his real name on my radio show there was no one more surprised than those the closest to him, Lilith and Eve. I'm not sure they knew who I was at the time, but they knew I was someone from the past because only someone from that far back would know what his real name had been.

I had already been raising eyebrows because of the info I had been releasing over the years since I started my radio show in 2004 and started writing articles and books. So they knew I was credible, they knew I knew what I was talking about.

But instead of being embraced by others for my knowledge and information I was put on assassination lists everywhere. They didn't want to talk to me, they wanted me dead. I was a threat to them because I wasn't one of them. Who is they? The Government itself. I was put on the 'black list' and even religious leaders wouldn't talk to me. Not one of them ever made an effort to contact me or get to know me. But they would mock me. They weren't short of excuses for that.

When the Father stood me up to speak for Him I wasn't embraced by anyone. My earliest memories of that time when I first started to speak out are of MOSSAD hitmen in my back yard. Welcome to the real world.

I knew the fight was on. Good thing Father had sent His Warriors because if there was something we had never done it was back down from a fight. And I had no intentions of backing down. I was just getting started.

Two million years after I was created Hallayel would start a war in Heaven that had never seen war.

At that time, Hallayel himself was about 6 million years old. He ruled over the 6th planet, Tiamet. And he was the 6th child created directly by Yahuah. An interesting correlation of 666.

Chapter Four

The Series : Interview
With The Devil - Part 1

April 22, 2016

Sherry - have you regretted anything?

    Lucifer - no, I'd do it all over again.

    Sherry - what about all the murders, sacrificing, the things you have done to humans on this planet?

    Lucifer -You know that made me so angry when you guys were recreating Shan and Father was going to put people in His likeness on that rock...what we weren't good enough for Him? We were the highest and most beautiful of the angels and He makes us feel like second class citizens? I was angry...I just wanted to destroy what you guys were doing down there...and I have....every day of every year of every century I have destroyed everything about that place...I don't care about babies, about women, about children, they're humans...I'll destroy them all...

    Sherry - have you liked any humans over the ages?

    Lucifer - there have been some humans that I've liked over the years, but not very many. Not very many....I liked Napoleon, I liked Hitler, I used to mess with him all the time he didn't know what was going on...I would just take over him like a Barbie doll...he had nothing to say about it..

    Sherry - What about Aleister Crowley, Anton Lavey, the wickedest of the wicked?

Lucifer - They were useful, Crowley was worse than me....they sacrificed Lavey to me and I met him down in hell...he expected a big hug or something, it was funny, he got what he had coming, they all do... they all know they're going to hell when they die so why do they think I'm going to save them from it? Because I said I would? You don't make a deal with the devil, you make a deal I break the deal...that's how it works. I'll spit and lie to keep those *uckers on my side, but when they die they're not mine anymore, they just go join the dead.. I have nothing to say over that.

Sherry - what about Adam Weishaupt (founder of the Illuminati) was he one of your favorites?

Lucifer - He was a little punk. I liked Adam.

Sherry - what do you see as the most dominant country in the world today?

Lucifer - They're all messed up, we control all of them.

Sherry - Which one do you see as coming out the strongest?

Lucifer - Probably Russia...they know how to keep their mouths shut and hide. America's just annoying. Too many fools in the hen house constantly walking in and out the door. We just got to the point we started replacing them all and controlling everything behind the scenes. We are the shadow government...we're the shadow government in every country.

Sherry - what about Israel? Seems you spend most your time in America?

Lucifer - America is where most of dad's people are...and that's why we want to destroy that place so bad. It's always been our focus...we already own everyone else...always have.

Lucifer - they all know who you are but they all hate you.

Sherry - they never stop trying to kill me...

Lucifer - and they never will...you're not one of us. To much light... they hate light...most of them are worse than me...you're all like candles burning on a cake and we just take out one candle at a time. the ones with the most light are our targets...if we can't get them on our side, we just kill them...

Lucifer - I don't care if you make this public, I've already won...there's nothing but crumbs left on earth you guys are fighting for....everyone's ours....

Sherry - but what good does that do you when they die they go to (Hell) the realm of the dead?

Lucifer - dad doesn't get them...that's what it does for me...every person I get is mine, and I got way more than Him.

Sherry - don't you worry about the Day of Judgment that's coming?

Lucifer - I'll find a way around it. I always find a way.

Lucifer - America is the birthday cake...it's more fun for us to snuff out the light...it's a numbers game now, we could rule the world now if we wanted to, what's the rush?

Lucifer - The thing with America, like you've said, is they are the real Israel...we want to rule over Israel...no one cares about Jerusalem, that's all our people over there...the real Israel is in America...even Europe...we own all them...we want Judah, and Judah is in America because you're there...

Lucifer - If you leave...game over, we just take over America and move on...add it to our collection..

Lucifer - While you're here...you give us to many problems...to much attention...

Lucifer - You're always trouble...because if you're around that means dad is too..

Lucifer - Both of his daughters right there in Ohio...the Orgone war, it's trouble...it's all trouble...

◆ ◆ ◆

Lucifer - The Middle East is boring...there's nothing going on over there that we don't already control..

Sherry - so what was the original Israel like, like the ones in Egypt were they black, white, middle eastern looking...?

Lucifer - slaves in Egypt ..yeah they were white, we've chased you guys from Egypt back to Israel over to the USA.. then we filled up Israel with Turks, hid the real identity of the Jews, and the rest goes from there, course you figured it out but no one listens to you...we make sure of that.. there's more of us that listen to your show than dad's people.

Lucifer - The world is controlled from NY...that's why the focus is NY and OH because you're there and dad's there...that's where a lot of action is for us...there's just a lot of stuff going on in that region.

Sherry - tell me something about the (rebellion) War itself...

Lucifer - the War...it last about 1,000 years earth time...you destroyed all the planets so we had to try and rebuild them...NASA hides a lot of it... they all do...you can live on just about all the planets still, Jupiter..Jupiter doesn't work in Earth's dimension...but in our dimension it's fine...the Orgone's destroyed space, you can't hardly live in it anymore...I don't know how you figured that out, but it's working against us....we just tell everyone you're crazy while everyone else is trying to kill you off the planet.

◆ ◆ ◆

Sherry - why do some of these (ancient) gods have boobs?

Lucifer - Buddha and Moloch had boobs because that was Lillith... Buddha was a representation of Lillith with the Chinese...a combined god/goddess ruler over them represented by the male (Lucifer), Chinese and Lillith...although it's mostly Lillith and the Chinese..

Sherry - yeah Father said Moloch the Baphomet, was Satan and the goat combined, with Lillith...the breasts...the combined female/male worship was Lillith and Lucifer,

some tidbits....

-whenever there's something combined male/female it's those two..

-the gene itself that makes people both sexes is a freak gene like the gigantism gene of hybrids, anomaly...

-angels aren't hermaphrodite

- angel swords are/were awarded to them by Yah Himself. He would bless and anoint them. There was a ceremony at the palace when combat angels would receive swords.

-angels can eat food but it's energy that sustains them. They're energy beings. The animals in heaven are the same way, energy beings.

- they (animals) didn't have to eat to survive, if they did they would poop but the chemical composition was such that it would be quickly decomposed into the ground and then the ground would restore itself.

- when Lucy fell, and Yah's angels left the planets, the planets were in a fallen state because Yah's presence left them as well. That's why they became defiled...poop everywhere from his crossbreeds, Lucifer digging into the insides of the planets and everything else...

- angels can eat, drink, and be merry, but the 'merry' part is much different from humans. There's a limit. They don't get drunk and stupid and belligerent or violent. They're energy absorbs alcohol, doesn't affect them like it does humans.

♦ ♦ ♦

Lucifer - the people in DC know you're legit...they've seen stuff...that's why so much of what you deal with is them, it's not even me it's them..

Lucifer - Even clones have memories. They think they're human. They don't know they're not...they think they are as normal and real as anyone else. That's why you have to watch them, especially people like him (Obama) in public positions...those you have to watch...they'll do or say something crazy...you can't trust them you never know what's going to happen. They could break down, malfunction, go haywire, they're unreliable. Obama thinks he's normal, he doesn't know anything different.

Lucifer - India, that was me and Eve. She had more kids with me after I was cursed but she hid them away...her and Lillith never cared about what happened to me...they still loved me, they remembered who I was ..they stayed with me.

Lucifer - I could manipulate an angel form so I would use that one at times, and human forms I can manipulate...but it's hard to stay in them very long and operate in that dimension...I do it when I have to, otherwise I just chill and watch behind the scenes.

Lucifer - from Terra (Shema) we could be on earth in 10 minutes.

Sherry - would you take over Obama?

Lucifer - yeah, Maitreya would to. I don't know how you figured that one out.

♦ ♦ ♦

Lucifer - the only way you keep control of governments is controlling how much they spend, and how they spend it....that's why my people are in charge of every government.

Lucifer - I left music a long time ago, became a politician. Manipulating stupid humans was more fun,

Sherry - why are there so many different personifications of the devil?

Lucifer - so people don't know what to believe..

Lucifer - Moloch is like me and the goat combined.

Sherry - why do you want them to sacrifice their children to you?

Lucifer - because they're heartless souls...they would kill their own children for their own greed, that should tell you something about humans...

Sherry - but they're your kids doing it?

Lucifer - laughs....yeah I guess you got me on that one...laughs..

Lucifer - when we would get dad's people to do it that was really funny...but even back then, as it is today, you have to teach them that to get you have to give. That's the whole concept, they always have to give....and what's really funny is if they ever stop, we just take everything they got away,

Lucifer -don't ever make a deal with the devil, you can't win, they can't win, they're just greedy *uckers and we exploit it...

Lucifer - "money is the root of all evil' they should have read their Bibles..

Lucifer - people who think they can play both sides are going to get burned by one of them....always take a side and be loyal to that side....

Sherry - So why do your ships always pile up in this region?

Lucifer - They just want to watch the show...

Sherry - are they engaging the angels?

Lucifer - not really...not anymore...we've lost so many they'd be stupid to try to...but they do what they want...sometimes when you see angels you just gotta have target practice...everyone hates angels...they're worse than humans...

Lucifer - some of you are just really hard core and we just can't get to you, you stay with dad no matter what, and that's why it's even still a war on earth for us...if America went down completely, we'd own the entire world. Plain and simple.

♦ ♦ ♦

Lucifer - Notable Quotes on the KJV

Sherry - Why was Enoch left out of the Bible?

Lucifer - Enoch...he revealed to much info..

Sherry - What about Jubilees and Jasher?

Lucifer - it was just easier to keep them out and go with the narrative we had.

Sherry - Why did you have just 13 books of Paul (and his associates) in the New Testament? Was that a specific purpose?

Lucifer - 13 books of Paul...that's code, that our influence is in it... we're in control...whenever you see our codes, it means our influence, we're controlling it..

Lucifer - You were right about dad's message being in it, but we control the rest...we edited things in and out to make it the way we wanted it not giving to much info. Enough to keep the people happy and convinced they had all that matters...

Lucifer - Paul was ours ..(laughs)...I don't know how you figured that one out...not many did, or will even accept it. We don't care, no one believes you except us, and what do we matter? It's your people that are deceived about him not us.

Lucifer - the KJV...(laughs)...why do you think we know it? Because we wrote it...we took over all their letters and combined it to give them (Jews) some history and keep them under our control. Religion is like politics. Give them something then control it.

(Lucifer talking to the Most High)

"There's some truth there (KJV)...enough to condemn people who don't believe it at all....but like with Paul, that was genius...and we use him for everything. Just like she's said that almost all false doctrines come from his teachings...she got that right, but no one cares about her.

I've listened to every one of her shows, I've listened to everything she's ever said, I've read every thing she's ever written...I have to say, good job, she nailed a lot of it, but like I've said a million times who cares, no one's going to believe her. We keep them so confused they all just hate her like we do. No one's worried.

We did a hack job on the Torah to but most people (real Jews) don't' realize it. That's why most of them rejected the KJV and kept to the Oral Traditions...course we got rid of all them. The ones now just believe it (Torah as it's presented in the KJV) and go along with everyone else. Time is always on our side."

◆ ◆ ◆

Global Warming – Flat Earth Theory – Straight from the Horse's Mouth

I just want you to see Perspective folks...it's Us vs. Them...you can believe us or you believe them, but either way you have to take sides in this war because if you don't Lucifer gets you on default as one of his own when you're cast into Hell when you die. He can't save you from that. He can't protect you from that. He has no power over that. Once a person dies they go to Heaven or Hell. It's your choice to make while you're alive here on earth because once you die It's TOO LATE to change your mind!

Tidbits from my first Interview with the Devil:

Sherry – Where did Nibiru come from?

Lucifer – Nibiru was my secret planet away from our own solar system...some of my people had set up shop on there and we used that as a headquarters to start our own stuff and meet at before the takeover started...we wanted to make sure everything was kept secret until then...we had planned this for a long time....and then like the perfect little presidential candidate I was I sold it to the other angels and the takeover began..

Sherry – When I asked Father about Nibiru He said, "Nibiru was a planet they were trying to turn into a 'sun' so they could mimic our heliocentric universe and create their own...with Nibiru as the center. I gave them plenty of time to repent, and then that time of patience was over it was the time of judgment."

Sherry – What about the flat earth theory? What is this crap?

Lucifer – (laughs..busts out laughing....) that's another one of our ingenious distractions ...it keeps the fools busy...

Sherry – like global warming?

Lucifer – (busts out laughing again...) hey it is hot with the Orgone...

Lucifer – you have to understand a lot of that is code amongst each other...then when they get caught speaking code they have to make something out of it and it just gets bigger and bigger then...

Sherry – the lie(s)

Lucifer –yes..

Sherry – so global warming's my Orgone... I knew it was..

Lucifer – (laughs)

Lucifer – flat earth doesn't even make sense, these people will believe anything..

Sherry –that was the original assumption that the earth was flat, they found out it was round and you were killing them off for that, now you got it back to being flat again...

Lucifer – (laughs) they got satellite photos from space showing a round earth…I don't know what else to say about that…people are fools… sometimes it's just to easy to manipulate and deceive them…to easy… when they're that dumb it just takes the fun out, Laughs…they'll believe anything I say just because I say it? I love that.

Sherry – yeah but they're parading the scientists in front of them, it's them they're believing…

Lucifer – it's still from me…

Sherry – was Jurassic park from Urantia? Yep…

Sherry – what about Star Trek? That was Ella on Jupiter?

Lucifer – yep. We got stuff from all those old places…you can see it all over earth now…in movies, in books, in songs, people think it's fiction and ingenious when they think that stuff up…and I'm the one giving it to them..

Chapter Five

Interview With the
Devil – Part 2

04-26-16

Sherry – So Sannanda said he's heading to the Vatican when he arrives.

    Lucifer – The Vatican, we own that place. I have my throne there.

    Sherry – I know, it's disgusting,

    Lucifer – ha! That whole place is "me", it's a shrine to me!

    Sherry – I posted something on the internet yesterday how it's the epicenter for child and sex trafficking.

    Lucifer – yeah they come through us first…we get our pick of the litter…that's the way it always is…then we just pass the others along.

    Sherry – so you are raping and eating children…

    Lucifer- I'm evil, I do it all, I could care less about stupid human babies, they're worthless to me…useless.

    Sherry – well they haven't had a chance to grow up…

    Lucifer – (laughs)…and they won't, who needs them, there's 7-8 billion people in the world and most of them are ours anyway…you go causing problems with your liberation efforts and *ullshit to free them from us, we own them..

    Sherry – no one owns another soul…only Father.

    Sherry – I'm not going to start an argument…either way the Vatican is where they're headed…tell me more about that place..

42

Lucifer – you destroyed the underground city we had under there...I was pissed!

Sherry- you lost it to me

Lucifer – screw your deals...you got D.C. and Buckingham too...you made a mess out of our little triage, it's so bad it's impossible to even try to rebuild them...there's no way to hide it, it would create to much attention.

Sherry – I don't always lose...you beat me down constantly but I find ways to win.

Lucifer – (laughs)...yeah you're good...I don't know how you do it... those people watching you don't know crap about how things work, they're useless idiots...only I could take you on and dad knows it, that's why He won't let me confront you on earth and play some real ball!

Sherry – (laughs)...I'm the limited one here, not you, I don't have anything here...you have control of the whole world.

Lucifer – apparently you've had enough...I've rounded a few corners where you've kicked my ass...and I never saw it coming...that was good... that was good...but you can't stop me, I'll still win...I'll win...and you can take your sorry angel ass back to heaven and just stay there.

Sherry – (laughs)....I can see you're in a mood today.

Lucifer – I'm sick of this place, we need to get things rolling...make things happen...I'm missing a lot of fun because I have to sit here?? Man, it just pisses me off.

Sherry – how's Lillith doing up there

Lucifer – same as me pissed about being here, but she's got some stuff to do and play with now so it's not so unbearably boring, but she misses her girls, she misses earth...she misses everything about just being back there and running things...

Lucifer – dad said you've been revealing parts of our convos online.

Sherry – I keep it real.

Lucifer – He told me some of it, I figured you'd try to make me look like some pansy douche bag, but you're not doing to bad, at least you're not changing my info, my stuff,

Sherry – I write it like you say it, I'm not changing anything…it's about your perspective, about mine, about ours, it is what it is, I'm not changing it everything's straight up.

Lucifer – everything's still from your viewpoint, but you can quote me, I don't care, I'm just responding to your questions.

Sherry – all I want is perspective, putting things in perspective…some of this stuff has been fascinating getting able to remember stuff from the past…we're not born with memories, dad doesn't give them to us …I bug him all the time about it, I want to know, I want to remember.

Sherry – I was listening to that song you wrote, "Wish You Were Here" (Pink Floyd)…

Lucifer – (laughs)..yeah…how'd you know?

Sherry – dad told me.

Lucifer – (laughs)…yeah I gave that to him (Pink Floyd band).

Sherry – He told me about Hurricane (Neil Young) to…you took my music and changed the lyrics?

Lucifer – (laughs)…yeah …yep..

Sherry – I can't even believe I wrote that music, but I've always felt a connection to it…I've always loved the guitar in that.

Lucifer – because you wrote it…you played it…that was from one of those ballads you wrote when you learned how to play…I told you, you were good.

Sherry – I was shocked.

Lucifer – (laughs)…we just bring it all down here…people don't even know…they have no idea…and you're going and telling them all this stuff? They're going to think you're crazy…but they already do, we make damn sure of it too.

Sherry – I'm beyond the point of caring what people think anymore, I don't think I ever have.

Lucifer – (laughs)…they have no idea, the real story, the minions of stories we could tell.

Sherry – well that's what I'm trying to do, reveal one of the greatest stories never told.

Lucifer – (laughs)…it takes me way back, but for what…we're in the here and now.

Sherry – well what is the here and now, let's see…you run everything, you destroy everything, (Lucifer laughs)…you're going to take 8 billion people to hell….and other than dad I have no way to stop you…I have very little support, practically no money, I don't even leave the house. I don't even have a passport. I haven't even had a vacation in 5 years unless you want to call orgoning NYC a vacation, it was a lot of work.

Lucifer – ooo you got us on that one…they could never find you.

Sherry- they were sitting in a car in front of my hotel directing agents dressed as New Yorkers and tourists out trying to find us, I stood there and listened to them talk and they never even noticed me…it was hilarious.

Lucifer-dad kept you guys invisible, Rocky about had a fit you orgoned his estate (Rockefeller)

Sherry – (laughs)…

Lucifer – Soros, Hillary…Wall Street, mid town…

Sherry – (laughs)…what about that night we were staying in Westchester and I woke up and my bed was floating above Manhattan?

Lucifer – (laughs)…yeah that was us…when we did finally find you… (LOL….laughs…laughs)…I was waiting for you to get out of bed and just splatter all over the empire state building or something…that would have been funny..

Sherry- probably why dad told me not to get out of bed…I listen to dad….

Lucifer – (laughing…laughs…...on and on and on….)

Sherry- oh you liked that one eh….

Lucifer – that was great, I loved that…that was the witches…you had no power over them, that was hilarious.

Sherry – I was sleeping.

Lucifer – (laughs)….

Lucifer- you ever go back there I'd hunt you down myself.

Sherry – I'm not worried about you…I'll find out where you are and throw some NY pizza at your window..

Lucifer – (laughs)

Lucifer – you know we have to meet sometime, seriously we do, face to face...just talk...have a convo like we are now...dad said the times coming when we will have a showdown of sorts...I can't wait!

Sherry-I can't either, bring it on, ...I've had time to prepare and grasp the fact you certainly aren't who you used to be, the angel you were, to the ogre enemy you are now...people don't understand how I could sit and even talk to you, ask you questions...but they don't know where we're from, they don't know our past, all I can say is the future is going to be epic, one way or another, whether I'm on earth or not, or leave and come back...it's going to be epic...I can promise you that.

Lucifer – you'll be Shaz again...dad wouldn't let me near you otherwise...He protects you on earth...He won't let me near you...He keeps the others away, He watches them...do you know how many times they (angels) stand behind you while you sit at your little stupid desk and write and say abominations about me?

Sherry – LOL...abominations? It's truth...it's all truth.

Lucifer – I don't like you either.

Sherry - (laughs)...

Lucifer – so let's talk about the here and now....you won't stop the child trafficking..

Sherry – watch me, I'll find a way.

Lucifer – (laughs)...we turn them into animals...

Sherry – they already are, most are already possessed.

Lucifer – (laughs)...

Sherry – what are they clones of clones? Soul scalped humans with reptiles trying to act human until they get into Milabs and go crazy...?

Lucifer – that's the fun houses...the Milabs...sometimes the last thing one of those kids see is a big old reptile in their face breathing in theirs as they die...we tie them down on tables and do whatever we want...sometimes we rip their legs apart or completely off just to get inside them.

Sherry – oh good Lord....Father help the children...

Lucifer – (laughs)...you have no idea how evil we can be...you can't even think to the levels we go...I already know...because I've heard your comments about it...and you're right...you can't even fathom the things we've done.

Sherry – oh my $%$^%^%%$#$#$%%YYT#   dad's telling me to hold my temper.

Lucifer- (laughs)...He told me to tell you what goes on...you want to keep it real? I'll keep it real...but you can't handle it.

Lucifer – (laughs)...did you run away already?

Sherry – no I'm here, dad's telling me to stay calm.

Sherry – if I could put a grenade between your ears right now I would.

Lucifer – (laughs)...

Sherry – I'd shove it right in your mouth and watch it blow.

Lucifer – (laughs)...

Lucifer – why do you care...they're our kids...we can do what we want with our own.

Sherry – and how many times have you crossed the line into ours?

Lucifer – it happens.

Sherry – yeah...I know it does.

Lucifer – (laughs)..

Lucifer – you know the meat hook stories?

Sherry – yes

Lucifer – they're true! (laughs)...

Lucifer – We've been shoving human meat into the food supplies for decades and no one knew, no one even thought about it. Now they're starting to wake up because that stupid rabbi didn't keep his mouth shut. But it's more fun when people know what we're doing. It's in your face then. It's even more fun than I thought it would be because now people know what we're doing and they're still eating the food we put them in. They can eat their own, I don't care. Or when we ship them to other countries, "here have some crushed up chopped up, spiced up good ole American burgers"...(laughs).

Sherry – omg..

Lucifer – (busts up laughing)…

Lucifer – when you work for me, and they all do, they do what they're told to do. If they don't we kill them and free up the spot on the roster. We keep lists of who is what, where, all the corporations work for me, all the chains, it doesn't matter what industry it is…what they're making, what they're doing, the CEO's are mine… we leave the crumbs and smaller ones alone but they get affected by us anyway because they buy from our suppliers anyway…the money just goes up the chain to us…

Lucifer – where'd you go

Sherry – I'm here…

Lucifer – you're quiet

Sherry – you don't think I would be?

Lucifer – (laughs)….

Sherry – this is disgusting, pathetic,..I don't know how dad has had so much patience with this…

Lucifer – He doesn't watch…He knows what's going on but I seriously doubt He sits around to watch the shows…in the past you guys always took off at night time, you knew nothing good goes on then…you were right…night time is my time…it's party time…and I've taught my kids, and my own, the same thing….when the sun goes down it's time to have some fun!!

Sherry – is there anything or anyone with morals in your world?

Lucifer – you can't have morals and be in my world…I only promote the worst among them…if you want to rise to the top you have to earn it..

Sherry – how do the women earn it? The women usually go through Lillith…they have their own thing going on…she'll turn them into vampires and whores, she'll have them eating babies we rape and destroy…and if they're around me I make them do the same thing…I'll even marry the best of them…I have hundreds of wives, no one gives a *uck…I do whatever I want…

Sherry – you hurt the women you're with, they all say the same things…you're brutal…

Lucifer – I can't help it…I get excited…I'm just an animal….

Sherry – do you destroy men to?

Lucifer – I have...I don't care who it is, man or woman, although I enjoy the women more...with women it's more natural, with men it's just animal...if I'm with a man I usually just kill him, women I can love, men are just pathetic little *itches who can't deal with my brutality...and it's just more fun to see them die...I do to them what they always wanted to do to someone else...I take the rapists and give them some of their own medicine...

Lucifer – anytime you're dealing with humans...you get that blood lust, you get that craze....it literally just makes you crazy when you see, taste, or feel blood..

Sherry – why is it, what is it about blood?

Lucifer – life is in the blood...without it you die...and I want to watch them die...if you see blood someone's dying, or going to...it just makes you crazy you turn animal...

Sherry – you are an animal...

Lucifer – yeah you know a lot of the times I simply don't care...I don't feel remorse, I don't feel their pain, I give them pain...and that's just how it is...

Lucifer – we have these places underground where we just hang people up and torture and rape them over and over until we break them... once they're broken we just kill them...I like to strangle them and feel their last breath leaving...then we just throw them on meat hooks for processing...put them right back where they came from...in the meat supply....

Lucifer – you're quiet again....(laughs)...

Sherry – you're such a disgusting, vile being...do your minions Sannanda and Maitreya act just like you?

Lucifer – they're worse than me...why do you think Sannanda likes the Vatican so much?

Sherry – omg..

Lucifer – (laughs)...

Lucifer – do you know what a special visit to the pope is like?

Sherry – no what?

Sherry Shriner

Lucifer – means you get to go to the Vatican and suck his dick...that's what it means...and I don't care who it is...if you meet the pope you suck his dick...that's the rules..

Sherry – that's sick..

Lucifer – (laughs)...you think about that when you hear of world leaders and celebrities going and having meetings with the pope...(laughs)..... they get taken to a private room and he shows them his dick and says "suck it"...and they do...then he'll listen to what it is they want or want to say, they might get 5 seconds, 5 minutes, depends what moods he's in,.. (laughs)...if it's more than one person at a time then they each get their own private meeting with the pope...(laughs)....

Lucifer – then they might get taken to one of the fun rooms...or dining halls...those are the fun ones...if you sit down for a 4 course meal with the pope you never know what or who it's going to be. That one movie where they show the guy eating a part of the other ones brain in front of him? (I think that's Hannibal) Where do you think they get this stuff? This stuff happens...already has, always will...the Vatican horror house...horror city...it's the best of the best of sheer horror...I love that place...

Sherry – I'm going to blow it up...when dad lets us come back here I'm going to blow it up...you can count on that..

Lucifer – (laughs)...

Sherry – I'm going to destroy that place and every other place you sit your ass in..

Lucifer – (laughs)...

Lucifer – it goes on if I'm there or not...I've told you, a lot of them are worse than me....

Sherry – where does Lillith go when she comes to earth? Does she go there to the Vatican?

Lucifer – she used to, she used to go to the underground city a lot before you destroyed it...but we just moved everything above ground, the city's blocked off, no one sees what we don't want them to..

Sherry – where does she go now since she doesn't have Vatican, D.C. or Buckingham underground cities?

Lucifer – she likes Balmoral castle...she parties with the queen...and they built her a castle in France years ago that she likes. She has her bitches go see her there..

Sherry – what about America?

Lucifer – there's some underground tunnels and stuff she likes in LA... and she loves to have fun in Vegas...she'll do some vampiring in Chicago because no one ever notices that stuff, or they just don't care and hide it, they know better...Chicago, Boston, NYC, ...Boston not so much anymore but back in the day that used to be a great place..

Sherry – does she go to Africa, Middle East...

Lucifer – she has fun everywhere, you'll see her influences everywhere..

Sherry – what exactly are her influences?

Lucifer – (laughs)...corpses...

Lucifer – she's like a cat, she'll play and toy around with her prey before she kills it...

Sherry – you mean torture and torment?

Lucifer- well you would call it that but she wouldn't...or I for that matter...(laughs)...

Sherry – so tell me what goes on at the White House...

Lucifer – the White House....

Sherry – they have an underground bunker there ...

Lucifer – well they always did, but then they had to dig out a new and bigger one because you destroyed the city we had under D.C....

Sherry – I asked dad to destroy them beyond repair to...

Lucifer – and they did...it's easier to build around them or build new ones, they left a mess, complete mess, it just goes beyond description what they did to those cities...(Destroyer angels)...when dad destroys something He makes it impossible to just rebuild...

Sherry – good..

Lucifer – underground bunker at the White House...they have an altar to me there...it's sealed off, secret and private area, there's a medical facility there where they clone and replace people as they have to...they can put them in the mind machine and it wipes their brain...(Bill) Gates made me that, I like that thing…I like playing with it…putting normal people in there and they come out however way you want them…

Sherry – that's the mind eraser?

Lucifer – yes, have you seen it?

Sherry – I've heard about it, I've seen it in the codes…wasn't sure exactly what it was, thought it was that device they supposedly have as shown in (movie) Men in Black…

Lucifer – (laughs)…yeah that's a smaller, more temporary version… it can erase a recent memory…my machine can erase a person's whole mind…

Lucifer – how long have you known about it?

Sherry – maybe 10 years, 12,

Lucifer – we've had it for over 20 years…we can control a lot of people with that thing, intimidate them…do as we say or you get the machine…

Sherry – is that what Pink Floyd's Welcome to the Machine is about..

Lucifer – (laughs)…no, that was in regards to something else, but it's fitting now with this too…

Sherry – didn't you write that song

Lucifer – (laughs), yep…I wrote it for one of my sons…I don't remember which one, can refer to all of them at this point…

Sherry – how many do you have?

Lucifer – probably thousands…

Sherry – do you have them on earth?

Lucifer – no…dad fixed it so I couldn't have kids with humans after Eve, otherwise I probably would have had my own continent full of them.

Lucifer – but a lot of the ones in space you destroyed were mine…they weren't just Lillith's kids I had them all over the place.

Lucifer- the altar under the White House is for special occasions… otherwise it's sealed off…there's an altar of Baphomet under Congress… if they get to that then they can move on to special occasions at the White House.

Sherry – what do they do at the altar?

Lucifer – sacrifice to me.

Lucifer – statues are always landmarks...they're maps...signs of things...you know the codes you know what's what, where...you learn that in the mystery schools...higher up masons and the higher ups in the others...it's all high level knowledge stuff, but I'm sure I'll be listening to one of your shows some day and you'll just bust out the info...you always do...I don't know how you figure this stuff out...it's amusing..

Sherry – because Father tells me...

Lucifer – (laughs)...wouldn't doubt it....it would have to be Him because you're not one of us...and this whole house of cards is going to come tumbling down anyway....after we snuff out the light in America we'll tear it down...and then we'll make it all ours...

Lucifer – you remember how Shan used to be with just the civilizations...we're going to turn it back to that...resurrect the old ones...

Sherry- you won't have time....America will be destroyed, but it will never be rebuilt by you...

Lucifer – (laughs)...you're so confident in your little plans...

Sherry- they're Father's...this whole earth's going to be destroyed and there won't be any place for you to run...

Lucifer – I always find a place to run...always...

Sherry – not this time...

Lucifer – we'll see about that...

...The Vatican is nothing more than a pit of Hell itself...

Father said, "they seal up the holes in a human skull and use the vessel to drink blood out of."

- they take a hip off skeletal remains and use it as a plate to eat food off of...

- all the cardinals serve the pope, they are sex slaves to him if he wants them...otherwise they all take part in the destruction of children and adults there...it's not just limited to children. Many 'missing' adults end up there every year on their altars and in their fun houses...

- their fun houses are various tortures, located in many rooms through-out the area or house....people on tables being dismembered, skinned, dissected, various experiments performed on them with acids, chemicals to rot the skin and flesh off their bones, whatever they choose...they like to slowly torment and torture someone so that they go in shock and die... and then they all laugh...that's their favorite part...to hear someone yell-ing for mercy, or just die in shock at the horror being done to them.

- tens of thousands have died there and it's Lucifer's home, his throne, his seat on earth.

- in America...the Mormon temple is Satan's temple in the west...he has a gold throne in the basement of it..

- he has a throne under the White House in the east...under the U.N is his global rule temple...

Chapter Six

Interview With The Devil – Part 3

04-27-16

Sherry – Lucifer..

    Lucifer – yes...

    Sherry- I can feel that smirk

    Lucifer – back for more are you?

    Sherry – yeah I want to ask you a few things..

    Lucifer – oh goodie...

    Sherry – let's pick up from last time...

    Sherry – I was talking to dad and He said,

- they seal up the holes in a human skull and use the vessel to drink blood out of.

- they take a hip off skeletal remains and use it as a plate to eat food off of...

- all the cardinals serve the pope, they are sex slaves to him if he wants them...otherwise they all take part in the destruction of children and adults there...it's not just limited to children. Many 'missing' adults end up there every year on their altars and in their fun houses...

- Their fun houses are various tortures, located in many rooms through-out the area or house....people on tables being dismembered, skinned, dissected, various experiments performed on them with acids, chemicals to rot the skin and flesh off their bones, whatever they choose...they like to slowly torment and torture someone so that they go in shock and die... and then they all laugh...that's their favorite part...to hear someone yelling for mercy, or just die in shock at the horror being done to them.

- Tens of thousands have died there and it's Lucifer's home, his throne, his seat on earth.

Lucifer – we don't discriminate, yep I love that place...

Sherry – that's nasty, that's sick..

Lucifer – it's my house...when you come to my house I expect you to be a good little guest and honor the host...

Sherry- and how do you honor the host?

Lucifer – by taking part of course, (LOL)...we have all kinds of activities, only good sports are welcome. Those who aren't could find themselves on a torture table...

Sherry- does anyone ever survive those?

Lucifer – yes, sometimes we just teach people lessons on those... and then let them go...but they have to be one of mine, one of my own... politicians, world leaders, whatever, no one else would be allowed or able to escape that place. It's the Hotel California there...you can check in but you can never leave without permission to.

Sherry – whatever happened to that hotel out in California?

Lucifer – I haven't been there in ages..

Sherry – so let's talk about the temple under the Mormon Temple in Salt Lake City...Sannanda used to hang out there a lot several years ago, not sure if he still does...

Lucifer – yeah, that was one of our places until you ruined it.

Sherry – laughs...

Lucifer – you destroyed that whole area!

Sherry – laughs...

Sherry – they say there's a throne of gold down there where they do prayers to the dead? What the heck's that about?

Lucifer – they recollect the demons from the dead, that left them when they died...we recommission them and put them back to work. A lot of times demons take off to do their own thing after the person they inhabit dies. We go after them...

Sherry – interesting...

Sherry – I noticed that the structure, the temple, is similar to the one they found on the moon, or is that Mars...

Lucifer – yes it was a smaller replica, let's everyone know it's mine... we were going to make it into a smaller Jerusalem type place but after you destroyed it we lost interest in that place..

Sherry – laughs...

Sherry – what about the temple in the UN...tell me about that place...

Lucifer – the UN...oh there's a mouth full...

Sherry – I know right...laughs....

Sherry – what's this about Sannanda using a submarine down the Hudson river to access it from under the island itself...is there a tunnel from the Hudson river over to the UN for submarines?

Lucifer – (angry)...I don't know how you heard about that...when you first mentioned that I was absolutely stunned...stunned....

Sherry – laughs..

Lucifer – there's a base under the Great Lakes...course you already know that because you've been trying to get to it for years...but sometimes it's easier for him to go to that base then take a ride over to the UN that way......

Sherry – what about that base under Central Park...the one that went from Mt. Vernon, to the Bronx, under Central Park...kind of spread out there....

Lucifer – I don't know how you found out about that one...but you had that thing on fire while you were still in NY...

Sherry – I know...(laughs)...we knew it was on fire...but it was an ancient base...ancient, there before NYC was even built...

Lucifer – that's where a lot of those meat hook stories originate from, was that base...and there was a movie about it...subway going there whatever..

Sherry- yeah I posted a clip of it a while ago on my Facebook, I don't remember the name of it...

Lucifer – yeah that was actually true, of course they sensationalize stuff because if you're on a trip to that base you don't get out and you don't come back...

Lucifer – that's a huge processing facility there...the processing is still there...we just rebuilt and recreated an area to use for it...despite what you did to the rest of the area...that was an ancient city...no humans were ever allowed there...they couldn't handle it...

Sherry – what else was there?

Lucifer – nests.. it was tunnels, nests of lizards, and other type beings to just live and hang out in...their home under the earth...they all feed off humans. Humans who go into any underground area in NY are just plain stupid..

Sherry – they say there's an entrance at Times Square to the underground super subway system...

Lucifer - yeah...how did you know that...because you like nailed the Times Square access...sometimes you're info is so dead on...it's crazy..

Sherry – laughs...

Sherry – I've heard of mole hunts and email sweeps in DC...people think I'm getting my info from people there or the military or whatever, amusing..

Lucifer – I wouldn't doubt it...the info you reveal is like bomb shells at times...that's why we have people watching you but you never even leave that fucking place...unless you go on the road for one of your little orgoning fiascos....

Sherry – only a fiasco for you...(laughs)...

Lucifer – for years they just couldn't figure you out...

Sherry- I never hid I was dad's, His messenger on earth...

Lucifer – everyone says that...no one believes that stuff...but you ended up being legit...they've been trying to kill you for ages..

Sherry – yeah, I know. I'm always dealing with their bs...I get tired of it...and I don't even see or know the half of it...

Lucifer – laughs...

Sherry- so back to the UN itself...tell me about that place..

Sherry – when I was in NY the taxi guy said the real UN building was across the street from the one on the sound, river, there...the one they show on TV...

Lucifer – they use both buildings...there's a tunnel underneath that connects them...

Lucifer – they were waiting for you there, you never showed up...

Sherry – I sent the others that were with me...dad told me not to go myself they were using facial recognition tech to try and find me...so the others went..

Lucifer – I knew they'd been there...that Kelly was with you she was supposed to kill you...

Sherry – that's so stupid...how was she supposed to kill me? Poison cookies?? Seriously? Poison doesn't' kill me...so they killed Kelly in retaliation for not killing me...? You can't kill me with your stupid poisons... they haven't learned anything in over a decade..

Lucifer – yeah well they got pissed at her and took her out...she wasn't doing what she was told to do...she was going against them...even led you right to one of their brain boxes in Ft. Knox...

Sherry – laughs...

Lucifer- they were pissed...

Sherry – laughs...

Sherry – we annihilated that place...

Lucifer – and even Rich was with you, that was seriously fucked up... we had 2 of ours with you...

Sherry – they couldn't stand each other...Rich always felt he was superior to everyone else...I wasn't even with him during that mission...I went off with Kelly..

Lucifer – I know, and they were pissed....I know Rich was...he was pissed...he had everyone there to watch you guys,

Sherry – I know, there was a few there before we even got there...

Lucifer – laughs...

Sherry – they had the local lakes and ponds near Ft. Knox all blocked off

Lucifer – laughs

Sherry – we still found a way...we still got it..

Lucifer – how did you even find out about Rich...how did you even know?

Sherry – I always knew...I was patient with him...finally dad told me to confront him and when I did it didn't end up well with Rich...

Lucifer – that was crazy....

Sherry – yeah it blew me away how that went down...didn't see it coming...didn't expect that...but whatever, dad has my back....

Sherry – he had one of those serpents in him...

Lucifer – yep, he was mine...he thought he was playing you and you blew him away by telling him you already knew...that floored him...man he was pissed, shocked, that was like one of those epic moments amongst the losers side...

Sherry – losers?...(laughs)...you'll see...you'll see...

Sherry – they were expecting him to be in NY with me and we didn't take him...

Lucifer – I know I couldn't figure that out, why you didn't take him..

Sherry – he was to much trouble, always to much drama with him. I didn't want to deal with it..

Sherry- it's peaceful now...course there's others hiding in the branches that think they're hidden, but I know who they are...

Lucifer – laughs...we have people everywhere...

Sherry – I know. I have my fun...I toy with them for a while...

Lucifer – and you yell about Lillith? You took a page out of her book!

Sherry – laughs... I don't even know her book....I do my own thing..

Lucifer – the UN is the gateway to the Vatican, you gotta go through the UN to get here...or there I should say..

Lucifer – there's an altar there...there's a whole underground area for me! It's like an assembly room with my throne in it...in the center is an altar...there's no Baphomet there because I'll go there myself...they can sacrifice directly to me...

Sherry – yeah I was thinking about that Baphomet thing, there's no way they could duplicate that thing…like you couldn't physically show up as that thing because it's a mixture of 3 different things, so it's basically just an idol to use because you're not around there…

Lucifer – right….

Sherry- does Sannanda sit on your throne when you're not around?

Lucifer – he has his own…I'd kill him if he did…

Sherry – with you gone do you think they're all having fun playing boss? Or fighting to be the boss?

Lucifer – depends if they even know I'm gone, I know the White House people do…depends if they kept their mouths shut or not. I'll be back soon enough…then I'll have my revenge on the idiots who didn't have my back..

Sherry- and the ones who do?

Lucifer – mmmm, I love them…they're truly mine…but the stupid humans aren't the ones in charge of anything…the real controllers are straight up my own people,

Sherry – the reptiles?

Lucifer – yes…

Lucifer – that may have backfired on me this time. I may have to change some things..

Sherry – what kind of atrocities take place at the UN…is it anything like the Vatican?

Lucifer – laughs…it's where we make men, men. If you come into the UN as a human with any kind of light, you won't leave with it…we'll snuff all of it out of you…see that's something you guys don't even pay attention to that we do…

Sherry – light?

Lucifer - yes…it annoys us…that's why they all hate you and know you're not one of mine…

Sherry – well I would straight up tell anyone I'm not one of yours… (laughs)…

Lucifer – words can be deceiving…but light isn't…you either have it or you don't…and those with light bulbs sticking out of their heads are clearly not ours….and if they come in that way we quickly snuff it out and get rid of it…and believe me it's a good riddance…

Sherry – so what kinds of things do you do to snuff out a person's light?

Lucifer – we make them have sex with us, or demons, we make them drink blood, sacrifice babies, eat them…

Sherry – oh good Lord…that's just so abominable…how could you sink to that level of depravity where you would harm a baby, kill a child, rape them and kill them like their garbage to do away with…

Lucifer – because to us they are….

Sherry – that's so inhumane…it's so…

Lucifer – we're not human…don't forget who we are…and if humans want to play ball with me then they're going to have to be like us, totally, they have to be "one with us"…one with me…I won't have it any other way….totally sold out or nothing at all….

Sherry – you make it so they can't be redeemed, no light at all,

Lucifer – that's why it's effective…that's one of the reasons we do it…

Sherry – I mean they could still be redeemed but it makes it much harder because they're so demonically infested…

Lucifer – laughs…we make light repulsive to them…we make all of you the enemy…and if they don't get on board with that at that point, we would just kill them or soul scalp them, as you say…soul scalp..

Sherry – what do you do with their souls when they're soul scalped? Do you leave them in the human and just take over the body?

Lucifer – sometimes…sometimes we have fun and put their souls in other things, or places…the military bases have more fun with that…when you revealed they put them in jars on shelves in Dulce Base there were thousands of military people that about had a heart attack…(laughs)… you pissed a lot of people off revealing that one..

Sherry – I was at Dulce…

Lucifer – I know I heard…

Sherry – were a lot of them freed?

Lucifer – at that point yes, but they just refilled them later...

Sherry - oh good grief...

Lucifer – laughs..

Lucifer – we find ways around you...took us a while but we found some...

Sherry – what was that, 2008..there were thousands of them we got out of there, dad freed them....

Lucifer – we got control of the base back, took them a couple years but it's back to ours now...

Sherry – transducers..

Lucifer – yep, how'd you know about that...

Sherry – I've known for a while, like I said we toy with you guys...but I've about had it with the child trafficking, that's the last straw. Keep your garbage out of this country. You own all the others take it there and keep it there. Don't bring it to this one. Israel doesn't want it here. America doesn't want it here. We're going to fight against it until they take it out of here...

Lucifer – laughs...we'll see...

Sherry – oh I was going to ask, what about the flesh eating plagues on all those involved with it? How's that working out for them?

Lucifer – flesh eating plagues, the leprosy stuff? Is that you?

Sherry – LOL..laughs...yep

Lucifer – I didn't know that was you...

Sherry – laughs..

Lucifer – you bitch...oh that was a good one...now that I think about it, I do remember you saying something about it...yeah I forgot about that. Temporals can't even operate past a week now...the ones taking temp human bodies, they aren't lasting at all...they're getting eaten up. With the humans that get it, we kill them and clone them and replace them... out of sight out of mind...

Sherry – what about all these politicians, political candidates who are being taken down to those Milabs and forced to participate in that garbage??

Lucifer – that's all run by the others…I got nothing to say about it really…they'll just keep replacing them if they have to…I heard that's been real fucked up over there..

Lucifer - flesh eating plagues…I didn't realize that was you…

Sherry – dad said it's affected over 10,000……(at the time of publishing this book it's over 91,000)

Lucifer – that's why I'm losing so many…

Lucifer – we may have to deal on that one..

Sherry – no deals…you don't keep them anyway…don't waste my time…

Lucifer – laughs…

Sherry – so what goes on, on the 13th floor of the UN?

Lucifer – 13th floor….? Hmm let me think….13th floor is where the mind sweeper is, the mind eraser, mind swipe, whatever you want to call it… that's where that is…we often have to use it on the employees to keep them in line…or entourages that come in. That's how we take control over all the countries of the world. We invite them to the UN…they come in thinking they have a pair of balls, we cut them off of them…they go to the 13th floor and get introduced to indoctrination my way…(laughs)…

Sherry – they feature it in one of those movies, I think it was one of those Left Behind movies.

Lucifer – (laughs)…yeah…it's been one of the best kept secrets….

Sherry – where else do they have them….

Lucifer – there's one in the Middle East. We found just doing whole populations with that thing just makes them idiots…so we blow them up in wars and start over…(laughs)….

Sherry – that doesn't even surprise me….

Lucifer – (laughs)…we cover all of our screw ups in wars…

Sherry – is that why America's been in war 200 years out of it's 300 years of existence? Covering your ass??

Lucifer – laughs…that and other things…American fighters are more reliable…they'll do what they're told, they'll do their jobs…they just want to get back home, it's worked out well for us….

Sherry – why don't you use the Russians?

Lucifer – they're always on a political back side, we keep them opposite America...so we can pull whichever side we need to do what we want...it's just strategy...we own them all, they answer to us...they do whatever we tell them to do...

Sherry – what about giving control of all the money to the Rothschilds?

Lucifer – we used the Rothschild's as the face of humans...to take control of the central banks in all the countries we wanted. They've been useful pawns. He knows it's all ours. We give him crumbs to keep him happy and to keep up the charade that some faction is behind it...

Sherry – what about the Bush's and the whole Nazi faction...

Lucifer – that's us, we had practice with Hitler and now everything we did to Germany we'll just do to America when the time comes to take it down. You always have to have a human face in front of something... that way they don't see us controlling everything in the background. But you figured out none of those humans are even human anymore....you and others have exposed a lot of what we are doing...we don't even care anymore, no one can stop it, no one can do a thing about it...that's why nothing is done about it...no one has the power to do anything about it... (laughs)...

Sherry – tell me about Diana's death, Harry and William's. I heard about those a long time ago...

Lucifer – Diana had real Jewish blood so Charles couldn't even stand it. He was supposed to have kids with her for the bloodline and throne connection. But then the boys were asking to many questions they were replaced. When you talked about that I about flipped my chair...no one even knew about the boys at that time...they were sacrificed...no one liked those little Jew boys...they had light...

Sherry – what about Kate is she a tranny?

Lucifer -.they all are...when you started blowing the lid off that I laughed....took you long enough...we get them when they're babies and start pumping them with gender pills...we got a whole slew of adults now that are tranny's...one of Lillith's games, having fun with deceiving people...it's right there in peoples faces and there's even videos exposing them for what they are and people still won't believe it...they'd call me a liar if I told them Michael wasn't really a Michelle....(Obama)..(laughs)...

Sherry – every time I expose celebrities for being one or the other the rag mags come out with stuff refuting it, to bolster their female or male sex appeal to make tranny accusations look like conspiracy lies...

Lucifer – that's what they do, and they'll always do it because we own the press and you're messing with someone's bread machine...those celebrities make a lot of people money...celebrities themselves get crumbs of what they actually make...when you mess with someone's bread machine they're going to fight you...

Sherry – what about Robin Williams, why did they kill him..

Lucifer – he sacrificed himself...he wasn't going to go any further with it. He wouldn't sacrifice his kids or anyone he loved. He told them to just take him and leave the others alone...so they did...

Sherry – what about Paul Walker ...blowing him up in his car...

Lucifer – you hit that one on the head when it all came out back when... that Vin Diesel guy was behind it. When you said that I was shocked... stunned you figured it out. Walker wouldn't join, so he became Diesel's sacrifice...and that was a good one for him because those two were best friends for a long time, they were close..."he was like a brother to me"... when he was saying that stuff because he was using it as like a family sacrifice (and letting it be known that's what it was)...the closer to family the more power you get from it. Family's always the most powerful kind of sacrifice...

Sherry – what about Prince? They killed Prince last week...

Lucifer – they killed Prince?

Sherry – yeah they killed Prince, Doris Roberts and that WWE woman Chyna...

Lucifer – Doris Roberts was one of mine!

Sherry – she was wearing red and black a couple days before they found her dead in bed...they say that's a giveaway for sacrifice...sacrificial colors red/black...

Lucifer – she sacrificed herself...she probably thought she'd get more rewards when she died...(laughs)...

Lucifer – Prince...he was a lab rat one of those Mk Ultra people...he was gay so they left him alone for a long time but he was fighting against everyone because they think they can, they think they'll be left alone and enjoy their own little lives and it doesn't work that way. When you're a lab rat we own you, we always own you....that's why we put them through the labs before they get to be stars, or musicians, they go through the labs. Or they sign the dotted line...and then we take them to the labs to start the programming, they have to learn the system, everyone answers to someone. If you break the system and end up on the outside, you get picked off, you get sacrificed, killed...to show the others what happens when you think you can break or leave the system..

Sherry- you put them all in prison...

Lucifer – we own everything, that's how we control it. We have structures of control everywhere, in every thing...even athletes have to answer to us now...

Sherry – Steph Curry was at the White House, is he Obama's new boy toy?

Lucifer – (laughs)...yeah I knew he'd like that one...(laughs)...

Sherry- what about Lebron James, Peyton Manning?

Lucifer – Lebron signed the dotted line, he's one of ours, he does what he's told, doesn't make waves, he wants rings, he'll spend his life chasing his possessions and then we'll take them all...that's how it usually works...(laughs)...

Lucifer – Peyton Manning, he signed...the famous ones who get media time have to...big contracts, media attention, only ours get approved for that...some come in under big contracts we just go after them later... if they want to keep getting them then they have to sign or join a club...if they don't they won't get another one...they just disappear into slavehood with the rest of the population or if they know to much we get rid of them in one way or another to show the others to keep quiet...you always need examples to intimidate the rest and keep them quiet, keep them in line.

Lucifer – if we want to keep their name going, their brand, we kill them and replace them if they're trouble…you can always make money off of or an example out of someone who was once famous and rich…it's just strategy..

Sherry – I can't understand them, how they could follow you, think it's an honor to serve you then go to hell for eternity…

Lucifer – (laughs)…out of sight out of mind, people live in the here and now, they want to get what they can now,

Sherry – such a waste, eternity is so much longer than the here and now…..

Lucifer – (laughs)…they don't see it that way…suits me fine…I take what's given…

Sherry – so what's on the 33rd floor of the UN?

Lucifer – 33rd floor is the Masonic floor, that's designed for the Masons… everyone gets their own playground in the UN for the religion they're in. We cater to them. We don't care what they come in believing but they'll leave kissing my ass…(laughs…LOL LOL). It's almost too funny now. I don't even care if people read this. It's funny to me. We're about to take over the whole world. America will be toast and we'll own it all. The light's at the end of the tunnel now so to speak…I don't know why you guys always say that, "follow the light at the end of the tunnel", the light's always bullshit…(laughs)…but whatever works…as long as it goes my way I don't care…(laughs)…

Sherry – Sannanda's supposed to arrive tomorrow, maybe today, it's really cold, he's got half the world under a freeze..

Lucifer – (laughs)…good..good…I'll be partying with him at the Vatican..

Sherry – and then what…

Lucifer – we snuff out America, force our chip into everyone and we win….we win the world once and for all, no haters, just everyone loving me…

Sherry – isn't Maitreya supposed to be the Antichrist and isn't he a half paraplegic about now…

Lucifer – I may have to take over him, we'll see how it plays out with him, I'll have to help him…

Sherry – this chip implant...the mark of the beast?

Lucifer – that's what you guys call it, we call it The Initiation, it's loyalty, I'm putting my stamp on my own, cattle branding...(laughs)...they're mine..

Sherry – what else does this do besides cattle brand them, does it tie them to a machine?

Lucifer – in a way yes, because we can turn them off...piss us off we kill you, we just turn the chip off...plain and simple...people will be crying "yes master" just to keep their lives...(laughs)...our slaves...(laughs)...

Lucifer – we can wipe out entire populations, killing people will be so easy...and a lot faster and more effective than vaccines....I can't wait for that....

Lucifer – the initiation into our Luciferian kingdom on earth...(laughs)... my kingdom...no haters, no light, Christians will be long dead and gone by then, they'll be the first ones dead as far as I'm concerned...since everyone else just follows us anyway and does what we tell them, not much resistance from them, it's the Jews in America, the real Israelites, the real Israel...they'll fight us but we're ready for it.

Sherry – you realize the Ark of the Covenant is in America...

Lucifer- hmmm. I don't need it...we can either play to deceive or just outright kill them off for dissenting, we'll see how it plays out but we have options...we don't need the ark, we don't need another temple in Jerusalem, we don't need props when we can just kill them off and get rid of them once and for all...

Lucifer – you destroy the little narratives we have playing out in the churches there...that's why we're going with other options now... you do to much damage to us...it wouldn't be so bad but everyone else follows your lead and takes your stuff and spreads it out there as well....

Lucifer – the worse thing you can do to us is pull them out of the churches because it takes them away from our control...our narratives, timelines, you blew the lid on the Masons controlling that...laughs.... you've done a lot of damage to us but no one listens to you anyway...

Chapter Seven

Interview With The Devil – Part 4

04-28-16

Sherry – Lucifer

    Lucifer – yes, miss me?

    Sherry – no, I'm just up and it's late and I'm going over stuff…

    Lucifer – laughs…

    Sherry – I wanted to ask you some things..

    Lucifer – as usual..

    Sherry – dad said after the queens destroyed and left their planets, leading 2/3 of the angels with them…they stopped referring to Hallayel as Hallayel…they disowned him, excommunicated him from the family…they wanted nothing to do with him…they changed his name…

    Lucifer- laughs

    Sherry – what was the name they called you?

    Lucifer – Halayon…because that's what I used for what is now Orion..

    Sherry- so we called you Halayon?

    Lucifer – yes..

    Sherry – ok, Father said, "I removed My Spirit from him and all those who fell with him. They were cursed and changed into a fallen state." So they lost their (angelic) wings, their angelic glow, aura, and persona, their light…?

Lucifer – yes I lost my wings, we all did, we no longer looked like you idiots...I was happy for that...

Sherry – laughs...we could say the same thing, we didn't want you looking like us!

Lucifer – laughs...

Sherry – Father said, "Tiamet became the Vatican City of his fallen empire...to hide his atrocities he dug into the planet and built an underground temple for himself...complete with conference hall and assembly room so his advisors could meet in secret.."

Lucifer – yep, we had to hide everything, and I started that when you were off on your little tour with Ella and her group...that's when we decided we were going to make our break, when you were gone...

Sherry – why did you wait till I left?

Lucifer – because you would have tried to stop us...you would have done something crazy and destroyed what we had set up...I didn't want to deal with that, and with you gone, Rashayel wouldn't be around either...course she was never around me anyway...but you were suspect of things, you were starting to get suspicious...asking questions, watching...so I knew when you left it was the time to make our move...

Sherry – go on, what did you do..

Lucifer – I announced changes in administration and setting up a new economy...I put my people everywhere and we just did what we wanted, we took over, and those who fought against us had no power against me, I was Hallayel...who were they??

Lucifer – the other queens attempted to stop me but I wouldn't even see them or I would brush them off and tell them this was what we were doing...they would huff off in anger, so what...

Sherry...Father said after what we call the fall of that time...or the rebellion...that you took for yourself the women angels who fell with you and impregnated them all..

Lucifer – laughs...ah yeah...LOL...yeah...yeah...

Sherry – that you took the wives of the male angels who fell with you and raped them all....

Lucifer – laughs...yeah...they had to prove their loyalty to me, if they could be loyal to me after I raped their wife in front of them, then that's loyal...course it also means they were stupid douchbags who couldn't protect their wives from me but whatever, I let them keep their dignity, called it loyalty and gave them jobs with me directly...set it up as a reward system for them...it worked out well for me, always has.

Sherry – Father said, "he got much joy destroying the spirits of those who adored him, then forced them to worship him while he mocked and laughed at their despair..."

Lucifer – LOL yep..

Sherry- --dad said, "he instituted palace and temple sex slaves... forced many of them to become his sex slaves...

Lucifer – LOL yep..

Sherry – ok, moving on...

Sherry – he said, "He raped the wives and daughters of his advisors and all those close to him in his administration and told them if they wanted to serve him they had to show complete loyalty by offering up to him, giving him everything they had in regards to loved ones and family members. He would make them his sex slaves and promote that advisor to the highest of positions in his empire or give them what they wanted."

Lucifer – yep, that's when I started the give-to-get model..

Sherry – model of what..

Lucifer – laughs...model of obedience, servitude, gratitude, you have to earn what you get, you have to give to get....

Sherry – who did you learn that from? How did you become so vile?

Lucifer – I can't even remember now...I just always knew that's what I wanted to do, that's how I wanted to run things and set up my kingdom...

Sherry- dad said, "He turned everything into a rewards system and forced them to earn what was once freely given...luxury homes, possessions, all had to be earned and rewarded. It was a feudal/class system of the haves and have nots."

Lucifer – yep, same way we do it now, but now it's harder to become a 'have' to begin with, starts with bloodline, goes out from there..

Sherry – Father said, "Angelic civilizations had to be rebuilt and restored. Those focused on technology and science were esteemed the highest while engineering and architectural design came in second. Philosophers, teachers, and economists were esteemed as well."

Lucifer – those focused on advancement...moving things forward...are always more prized by me...I love inventions and new stuff,

Sherry – you blew up Atlantis...

Lucifer – laughs...

Lucifer – no YOU blew up Atlantis...

Sherry – Shaz blew up Atlantis?

Lucifer – yes.!

Lucifer – of course they were idiots, blew half the place up misusing crystal tech they were developing, you finished them off...you sunk the entire continent!

Sherry – that was probably Rashayel...laughs...

Lucifer- probably, I don't care, you 2 were disgraceful...the things you did to me and mine!

Sherry – laughs...

Sherry – good...

Lucifer – we tried to resurrect it while dad was playing in the Garden of Eden...

Sherry – the Atlanteans, isn't that who the South Americans are from? Or was it just the Indian tribes of North America..?

Lucifer – I don't know how you figured that one out!! That was the bomb shell of all bomb shells!

Sherry – laughs...

Lucifer- it's actually a mixture of both...and they crossbred with those in India, Eve's kids...my people were everywhere acting as gods among the sheeple, then after the flood we had to start all over again...

Sherry – tell me about the flood...

Lucifer – we preserved a lot of our own people, not a lot but enough to start over again...we took them off the Earth and some found our tunnels and caves into the earth from Shan days and hid in those ...the Bible says the flood wiped out the entire population other than Noah but that wasn't true, we were able to help some of our own survive, we had them everywhere, we had to frantically go everywhere and pluck them off the ground ourselves...of course when I first started to see the rain I knew that was it...we got busy then with evacuations as we could...

Lucifer – I saw you and Rashayel... I knew it was going to be trouble... we got out of there, we got what we could, who we could, we got out...

Sherry- wasn't there dinosaurs at the time?

Lucifer – yes, but they were over in America, that was our little playground for crossbreeding those things...

Lucifer – there was like 1,000 years of nothing after you guys created Adam...it slowly took off in population but that first 1,000 years was just set up for everything that would happen later...obviously...

Lucifer – back then the land masses were larger, not so broken up as they are now...we divided it all up in sections ourselves, then the flood wiped everything out, we all had to start over again, that stupid little ark was hilarious...I don't know why you guys just didn't evacuate them off the earth at the time if you were going to destroy it? We all laughed...that was totally hilarious....we figured you guys just must be having some fun or something...

Sherry – we saved hundreds of animals, they needed caretakers....

Lucifer – laughs... could have just started over again,

Sherry – dad didn't want to, He had it planned the way He wanted it...it kept the continuity from the time of creation, Earth was only given a certain allotted amount of time and it kept the continuity going...and that's how He wanted it...

Lucifer – whatever, that was stupid and hilarious...whatever.....LOL...

Sherry – where did you take your evacuations to..?

Lucifer – Mars...some went to Terra, between those 2, we got about 5,000 off the Earth...we didn't have much notice. I just knew when I saw water to run!

Sherry – LOL...laughs...

Sherry – that was smart...LOL...

Lucifer – I saw you sitting on a mountain with your arms laying across your knees, just sitting there watching...you were talking to Rashayel, she was laughing....you were shaking your head...you looked shocked, angry and happy all at the same time...you guys call me crazy all the time? That was you two.....you were always doing something crazy...when you guys were loading up the ark I saw you riding giraffes, elephants, lions, navigating all the animals towards it, you guys were laughing, having fun....someone should have got that on tape! I know Lillith saw stuff...but she was getting busy with evacuating her kids because you told her you were going to destroy Earth...she knew you would...if you said it, you were going to do it...she had no doubt...watching the animals being led to the ark was the icing on the cake...

Sherry- ok so back to Tiamet, as much as I love talking about the flood era...I need to get back to Tiamet and close the chapter on that because dad said Vatican city idea was from Tiamet...

Lucifer – yep...I had to learn to be secretive back then, so I had it down for when we built Vatican City! That was the first real place on earth that I built after the flood era that was truly mine...you guys had no idea, no one did...but even back in the time of the Roman emperors and Jews being little slave bitches in Egypt and then dying in the desert I was building my palace at Vatican city...away from the politics of Rome....so they didn't know what I was doing...but I corrupted them all...I'd bring them over to my house and be the good little host that I always am....it goes way back...way back...

Sherry – did you have an altar on Tiamet?

Lucifer – yep...

Sherry – you sacrificed on Tiamet!!???

Lucifer – not the extent it is now, on Tiamet it was used for men offering their wives and daughters to me! I would take them right on the altar! I would make them watch! It was an altar for offerings...then...on Earth I changed it...because I hated humans so much I figured why not make it more of a useful platform...kill the stupid bitches...sacrifices were implemented for everything...Lillith was genius with all the stuff she came up with...

75

Sherry – were there a lot of families back then...I don't remember a lot of details...

Lucifer – yeah, angels could have sex...I don't know where people get the ideas they do about what it was like back then...angels had families... but it's like you've said, a lot didn't, a lot couldn't, and those who could, did...it was a mix...people think we were fairies or robots or something... it was a lot like Earth...we made Earth like it was back in our day but it's a lot more limited compared to that of course...but we had a lot of freedom and people don't understand that...like you always say they think we were sitting on clouds playing harps...

Sherry – probably because of the limited view you left in the KJV about it...

Lucifer – laughs... it was never a narrative on the past...not that far back...laughs...

Sherry – you said you did a hack job on the Torah and all the real Jews rejected it when the KJV came out...

Lucifer – laughs..yeah..

Sherry – did you change the calendar from solar to lunar?

Lucifer – yeah that was one of the things they were mad about...and all the nit picking details with 1,000 laws...it's really much simpler than what we made it sound like in the Torah...laughs...we made it impossible, no one could keep all that stuff....make is so complicated they give up and walk away...well either way they did...we buried stuff, we made it hard to understand...that's why most people can't even read it, even today...we made it sound much more detailed and judgmental than it was...most of it refers to temple priests and not the people themselves, we made the whole thing cumbersome ...hey that was my song (Cumbersome sung by Seven Mary Three), did you hear it? Laughs...

Sherry – yes...laughs...

Lucifer – I wrote that for you years ago...

Sherry – so I heard...

Lucifer – then I gave it to whoever, they trickle up, down, or over, depending where I am at the time...

Sherry – where do you spend most of your time when you're on earth?

Lucifer – Vatican probably…

Sherry – they've been reading our convos…

Lucifer – who?

Sherry – White House people…they hack my emails…I send them to Rashayel..

Lucifer – laughs…yeah they watch you like a hawk…

Sherry – I know.. I could care less…

Lucifer – laughs…

Sherry – they loved 2 of your notable quotes…

Lucifer – which ones…

Sherry – they liked the comment about when you said I could take my sorry angel ass back to heaven…

Lucifer – (busts up laughing)…LOL…LOL..so true, truly….LOL..

Sherry – and they liked that one about if someone has a light bulb sticking out of their head they're clearly not one of yours…

Lucifer – LOLOL..yep…LOL…yeah…..yeah….

Lucifer – well they would, those are my folks…

Lucifer – they hate your sorry ass…laughs…LOL…

Sherry – I could care less…

Lucifer – laughs…

Lucifer – that's funny…

Lucifer – do they have any idea how much time we spend talking to each other, or how much time you always talk to dad?

Sherry – no, not unless I write something and put it out there..

Lucifer – laughs…

Lucifer – you talk to Him a lot more than even I thought you did,

Sherry – how do you know…

Lucifer – because I know when He's talking to you…I can feel His energy to you…it's crazy..

Sherry – we're close..

Lucifer – laughs….awe, are you daddy's little girl?

Sherry – always have been…

Lucifer …laughs…

Lucifer – when you come back as Shaz it's going to be epic…epic..

Sherry – I can't wait…I'm sick of this body, and this shack on the hill…

Lucifer – laughs…LOL…yeah that's crazy…LOL…I never would have thought of that one…

Sherry – I got done what was needed…I got done what I needed to do here…you haven't seen the half of it yet, but you will…laughs…

Lucifer – I'll be the first one to hunt you down if you come back here to earth…

Sherry – you won't have to hunt me down, I'll be a hemorrhoid on your ass…I'll be in your face….I won't be hiding anywhere…I can guarantee you that…

Lucifer – laughs…

Chapter Eight

Interview With The Devil – Part 5

The Awakening

For a long time I had the majority of my memories blocked. I knew who I was and where I was from but there were so many details I just couldn't remember. The few memories I had of growing up in Heaven were priceless to me and enough to keep me going when so often I just wanted to give up.

As I started doing this series of Interviews with the Devil more and more was being opened up for me to remember. Father would reveal things to me and helped guide me through this whole process.

The most shocking aspects to me would be the rebellion itself and why and how it happened. I couldn't remember much of anything and what I did just didn't make sense because it didn't put the whole picture in front of me to see.

And then it finally happened. Father finally lifted the veil so I could see it. He revealed to me with Hadassah exactly what had happened during that time. Finally, I was getting an awakening, a breakthrough of information that would help me wake up and remember the things that had happened and taken place. It was shocking...because even though I was there at the time, as a human born on earth I was hearing it for the first time.

And when you read and learn for yourself what happened...you will realize that nothing new does happen here on Earth. As Ecclesiastes states there's nothing new under the sun.

Ecclesiastes 1:9-10

9 The thing that hath been, it is that which shall be; and that which is done is that which shall be done: and there is no new thing under the sun.

10 Is there any thing whereof it may be said, See, this is new? It hath been already of old time, which was before us.

There's nothing happening that hasn't happened before. That's eye opening when you put it into perspective with the information to be able to do so. Just shocking, and eye opening, and epic to see that everything happening around us now on Earth, already happened once before, in all places....Heaven. More specifically, Tiamet. Lucifer's planet of rule.

At some point, things started going terribly wrong with him and none of us knew exactly when his total rebellion against Father had started but Father Himself. And Father never told us. But He knew, and He watched him while we were busy doing our own things and taking care of our own responsibilities.

I often thought that the rebellion officially started when I had left and Lucifer decided to take charge over everything and make administration changes on all the planets. But it had started way before then. As Lucifer himself had told me "we planned it for a long time."

And he wasn't just planning he was preparing. He was beyond the drawing board and into full scale implementation at every level. Ones we couldn't even dream existed. We were blindsided, completely, he was cunning and calculative and when it came time for execution it had been well planned and implemented with precision. We were completely shocked.

I finally just asked Father directly, "What I want to know is why we just walked away from our planets?? Why we gave up our homes to that scoundrel and even let him have them to begin with? Why didn't you allow us to just kick him and his off our planets and even solar system altogether at that time?

Father – when you were gone, he had up to 50% of the populations with him...he was a great orator on putting in a new economic system, new system of elections, rehabilitating everything and into a new system and order of things...much of what you have in America now that you see doesn't work...it's easily corrupted to be controlled by the few...but the angels didn't see that...they didn't know of his crimes he kept hidden away at his temple inside Tiamet. They didn't know his true nature that was coming out at that time. He was zestful, charming, he sold it to them all...but my girls, nor my son, were fooled and they were angry. He took over with most of them (angels) supporting him at the time...you, Ellashayzor and Brianzianna were gone at the time. He took over your three planets and had full control of them by the time you came back. It was subtle...when you came back you were very angry and rallied against him...his revolution was turning into a war...

Sherry – evil only triumphs when the good people do nothing...so I want to know what it was that was so overwhelming that it would cause all of us to just walk away from our homes and then destroy them in our anger? If we walked away it was in defeat. Defeat of Hallayel?? How was that even possible? How was it he won? He won by us leaving...there had to be something so invasive, so evil, that we wouldn't stay...even if we had kicked all of his people off our planets themselves. I want to know what that was....

Father – as quickly as he had taken over the planets...he began to implement a system of punishment for those who were listening to you and the others, he was desperate to hold onto control and began using devices they had developed against the people....

Father – he gained control of the armies...while many fled, many were taken over by him as well, and became robots (like being chip implanted and controlled),...defending his empire against the righteous angels that were there....

Father – he would corrupt them, defile them, then take over them....just as he's done on earth...he's doing nothing new there child, everything you see down there now, is what he did in the past..."nothing new under the sun'...

Father – that's why you have so many memories of rescuing angels... you were rescuing them from his imprisonments he set up all over the planets...it was a war child..

Father – when he said he had planned it for a long time, he had...and when they made their move it wasn't just to deceive and manipulate... they had technological advances they had created and developed and used those against the people...en masse....

Father – the brainwashing techniques taught to the Nazi's were nothing new, the MK Ultra programs you have now, existed in the past, developed way back even then, that's how he took control...they kept it quiet and away from all of you...they were using Nibiru as a home away from Tiamet, all his scientists were there busy recreating angels to make them controllable...the 'mark of the beast' is nothing new, he did it back then... he incorporated it back then...

Father – Nibiru was his Dulce Base, Los Alamos...Milabs...

Sherry – why didn't you stop it?? Just end it before it even started?

Father – I can't inhibit free will. I can punish it, but once something begins it has to play out. Mankind was created with free will...so were the angels...

Father – he opened inner-dimensional doorways, gates, gateways...

Father – he had 18 million at the time of his revolt...creatures he brought in and trained to be military soldiers..

Sherry – you mean like with CERN?

Father – yes...

Hadassah – he brought in all kinds of evil spirits, beings, and he would brand them as his own and force them to work for him...

Sherry – like Solomon did with the demons?

Father – yes...he brought in thousands of them at a time, and one by one branded and took control of them...separated them into groups... then gave them portions of the planets to guard...

Hadassah – he put them over the prisons...to intimidate the others... what you know as Hell in earth...was where he would have these gates, he hid them well...he would pull these beings into "hell" and take control of them there...he would mind erase them, turn them into whatever he wanted, his robot armies, they were ugly, they were creatures from who knows where...he would target a particular area in the universe and if he could use those creatures he would pull them in through his gates....

Hadassah – he loaded the planets up with these creatures...when that started we all left...there were millions of them...he would laugh and unleash them onto the planets. He had gates on all of them...they all worked together...no one knew what was going on...he had set up secret places on every planet and dug into them and worked from the hollow centers of them...we had no idea...when we found out we were furious... that's why we left, those creatures were everywhere...you and Rashayel led the exodus off of them....we were literally escaping, not leaving as much as escaping the horror that was being unleashed on the planets. That's why after we left we destroyed them and kicked them out of our heliocentric system into where they are now.....he could sit and rot in his own mess...we all left...

Sherry – CERN"s not even original....

Father – oh no he had that in the past, he just recreated everything here..

Father – when the veil is lifted and the dimensions merge, it will be a recreation of what happened in the past...

Hadassah – we had stuff mapped out in the universe and his people stole the maps and used them for themselves. They'd pull in what they could control and use...

Hadassah – the last straw was armies he had coming from Nibiru...no one was prepared for that. We were trying to take control back of our own planets and seal off what he had going on inside them...but he had stuff hidden and gate entrances everywhere we couldn't even find, or knew about...it was a total onslaught, no one was prepared for it.

Hadassah – and the whole time...he just laughed...tried to act like he was some kind of military commander...it was pathetic...you see how Hitler was down there? That was Lucifer...totally...he would do the same stuff...line up all his armies and have them drill past him, or ride up through the center of them....he would do the exact same stuff...and he told you he took over Hitler and loved that guy, that's why.

Hadassah – he reenacts the past through dictators down there. Your history books don't reveal at all what's really gone on down there...

Hadassah – the creatures brought in diseases...people were getting sick, the animals, the planets...vegetation...everything was getting affected one way or another...

Hadassah – because he brought those creatures in, and they were evil, dad's glory and presence left the planets...and when His glory left them, we left...there was nothing to stay for then.

♦ ♦ ♦

Sherry - after we left the planets and kicked them away from us...how long did Lucifer operate on those other planets with what was left of them and all the chaos of those creatures?

Hadassah - he had a whole era, dad says about 1,000 years your time. We set up angelic posts around the sun and kept him and them away from it. Battle lines were drawn.

Hadassah - every once in a while you would go see him...confront him...other than that the only time we had anything to do with those planets was if some of our own were captured by them and held as prisoners...then you would take a group and go free them...not that you needed a group...(laughs), but whatever,...

Sherry - so that went on for 1,000 years...

Hadassah - then after that dad had a meeting with Lucifer...and after that, he gave you guys the permission to destroy those planets. You practically obliterated them. Lucifer knew it was coming and had run to

Orion...the rest weren't so lucky...a lot of the people he left on Tiamet and Shan etc...were loaded up onto Nibiru and cast out of the solar system...it became a prison planet...

Hadassah - and you guys were allowed to completely blow up Tiamet and blow it into smithereens...and you did..

Sherry - that's the planet I keep seeing that we split in half?

Hadassah - probably...laughs...course you've done that to a few, and star ships...laughs...

Hadassah - Tiamet is a layer of rocks now floating around out there in space somewhere...laughs...

Hadassah - the rest were pounded with hailstones and fire, some were pounded then flooded where they iced over...

Sherry - how many left to get away from Lucifer?

Hadassah - 21-23 billion left those planets...they went to Pleiades...we kept Mercury...we set up outposts around the sun...

Hadassah - what you did with Shaziron and Shazandro was epic...totally epic, everyone was so shocked...that was a huge epic bomb shell for everyone up here...good job sis!

Sherry - thanks sis...

♦ ♦ ♦

Sherry - Father you said Lucifer incorporated the mark of the beast during that time...can you tell me about that?

Father - it was something similar to what he will do down there. He forced all of the ones who supported him to show their loyalty to him by getting a stamp on the back of their hands, their right hands. He tried to promote it as entering a new era and told them that only those with his stamp of loyalty would be allowed to live on the planets and participate in his new kingdom of heaven. That really infuriated those who loved Me and knew he was out of line with his boasting and lying.

Father - at first most were intimidated into supporting him because they thought that's just what they should do since he was a prince of heaven. When the queens started to argue and fight against him on it he got more brazen and bold, and forceful.

Father - it was a stamp with his picture on it. Much like you would refer to as a tattoo down there. The currency he had was coins with his picture on them. Many were upset they would have to carry around coins for things and that everything would cost money to buy what had always been free. He was confusing everyone, making most angry, and no one wanted changes but those closest to him. He did away with our rewards system and appealed to the angels they could just buy what they wanted instead of having to earn the more luxuries of heaven. Before it had never been a focus of anyone's attention to have more and more and more, people were already content with what they had...he made them feel inferior and that they needed more, bigger, better, things. He was introducing materialism, greed, lust, jealousy, envy, just all the things contrary to the way things were.

Father - what scared them was he was threatening to kick people out of his kingdom who didn't get the stamp of loyalty. People didn't want to lose their homes and be uprooted from their families and communities, or lose their elected positions or service work (jobs). The queens continued to fight against him and contacted Ellashayzor to get back home with you and Brianzianna. Lucifer's revolution had begun. It happened quickly. He had planned every detail and when he started to implement his plans he did it forcefully and with authority that I had never given him.

Father - he showed no respect to the queens...but he knew to fear you because you never demanded respect you had already earned it from everyone in my kingdom. Everyone loved you and they would listen to you and Lucifer knew when you returned he was going to have problems with you. You were a mighty gladiator, strong, beautiful, charming, smart, the youngest yet the most fiercest with a commanding presence. He knew you would give him problems, and you did. You gave him a war.

Sherry - where was Yasha during this time?

Father - when Lucifer started his revolution Yasha was recalled to the Palace to be with me. You worked with him and he directed you in what to do and how to proceed with and against Lucifer. I would not allow Yasha to take him on directly. It was you I stood up. And you lead the angels as Yasha directed you. You and Yasha have always been very close. It worked out well and Lucifer lost most of his support even with his threats and violence against them but he would destroy most of the heavenly planets in the process and when evil invaded them with the millions of creatures he brought in as an onslaught, then you and Rashayel led the exodus and the majority of angels left them.

Sherry - what were these creatures like?

Father - hideous, ugly, grotesque, their very presence was an abomination. Lucifer had appointed leaders over them and they would harass the angels just by causing mayhem everywhere. If an angel had a stamp they were left alone, if they didn't they would try and bully them into getting it. Most of them had unnatural voices that were implanted into them to cause them to speak. Most angels would just fly or run away from them, some would be captured and put into prisons that had been set up by then for resistors but when you returned you began to destroy those with Rashayel and lead the exodus off the planets to the Pleiades.

Sherry - I cringe when I hear that name because the New Agers have cornered the Pleiades as if the Pleidians are making contact with them and leading them into their nefarious teachings and doctrines.

Father - There were some from the Pleiades who had left and joined Lucifer's side over the years but they are no longer mine. My angels don't come into contact with mankind to teach them anything, or lead them into anything, those are deceivers and Lucifer uses them to deceive people into the New Age lies they have been promoting. It will lead into the arrival of the beasts that are coming to earth as prophesied. Lucifer uses them because they look like angels, unlike his people who have been cursed and look like reptiles and snakes, along with Lilliths almond eyed races all over space and the various ones who have been manufactured and crossbred.

♦ ♦ ♦

After a while, we got tired of chasing down the creatures who would capture angels and hold them captive...so we created these big nets...and we would go capture them and put them in these big nets. We would get thousands of them inside the nets then set them on fire and destroy them.

Me and Rashayel would just go out and collect them, round them up... and then burn them. Ella and Branz made us these things that resemble vacuum hoses and light beams that we could use from our air pods making it much easier to collect them in huge groups at a time.

We could target the frequency signature of the beings and then do sweeps for them. We organized clean up crews to go through and sweep space, and the planets, of all these creatures.

And of course Lucifer was furious and they would try to confront our ships to prevent us from getting near their ships and planets.

So that's the bulk of the war, trying to clean up his mess and battling him from preventing us to. We got the bulk of them.... and at the end of 1,000 years most of space and the planets and star ships had been cleared of the creatures that had taken over them and inhabited them.. Dad then gave us permission to obliterate the planets in judgment. Lucy ran to Orion while all the others were collected onto Tiamet and Nibiru. Tiamet was blown out of existence and Nibiru became a prison planet and was thrown out of the solar system. Nibiru was the bulk of Lucifer's wives and kids and the other angels who were secondary in his rebellion against Father.

Those on Tiamet were his administrators, administration, his top tier managers, all those involved directly with him...the entire planet was destroyed by fire and then blown up.

Shan and the other planets that had been used by them were pounded into oblivion with huge hail stones of fire and then flooded putting them into ice ages...with the deep freeze and ice ages killing anything off that had survived up to that point.

Chapter Nine

Interview With The Devil - Part 6

04-29-16

(Previous discussion with the Most High (Father) and Hadasseh on "The Rebellion and War" Lucifer initiated in Heaven) The Pleiades were put together and created as heavenly planets very quickly...they would become replacements for the Heavenly galaxy Lucifer was in the middle of destroying with all his interdimensional, cross dimensional creatures and nonsense.

Lucifer - those were put up quick...you guys were taking off to those in droves, Ella was using her transporters and running them constantly back and forth, most of the little air pods we used in our galaxy weren't suitable for long trips to another one...so everyone had to be transported over, and of course they wanted to take their possessions and everything they could...it was quite a project for you guys but I left it alone, I didn't need any grief from you...you would have been pounding and pouting all over my house (palace/city) and I didn't need to deal with it...it wasn't that important, you guys were leaving, good riddance...

    Sherry - yeah you probably had stuff you were hiding and didn't want me to see, or find out about...or burn down....

    Lucifer - laughs...yeah well with you you never knew what you would do...it was diplomacy or a fight, or complete war, you change with the wind...unpredictable....always unpredictable..

Sherry - laughs...depends how mad I am, or get, or what dad tells me...

Lucifer - yeah well, you've always been the one no one wants to mess with...you have reputation...you're a legend in space...everyone's heard of you, ...you have no idea being stuck on that rock...you don't even remember who you are, but I'm glad dad's letting you remember now, it makes things easier. I hated waiting for the bomb to drop because I know the bomb shells are coming...and they're going to come...I know that...I'm tired of looking over my shoulder, I'd rather have everything in front of me...

Lucifer - your little Orgone war blindsided me...then you somehow managed a revolution in space, total revolt...from that little rock you're stuck on...in your little shack...that was a bomb shell, that was absolutely stunning...I thought your little war victory in 2012 was bad...you completely stunned me on this one...

Sherry - laughs...

Lucifer - then when that settles down, you end up turning around taking almost the entire Andromeda galaxy, dad said 90% !!!!!!!! That's crazy!!!! They weren't our people but that was still shocking...They were always friends with the Pleides anyway...just no one ever thought to assimilate them as one of their own, or thought it even possible...you made it happen and that was epic...that was epic....

Lucifer- how many did you get ?

Sherry - with both? 19.2 billion total...

Lucifer - wow, not surprising...but wow, you like the blindsides, I know that....

Sherry - I got more coming...laughs....

Lucifer - I will kick your ass...

Sherry - laughs.....

Sherry- this little shack hasn't been to bad, has served me well, allows me to focus on things that matter other than things that don't...I like being out of the way, alone, it has served me well.

Lucifer - I used to think you were so pathetic, now it's just genius... genius...

Sherry - no one took me as a threat...till it became to obvious to ignore, but the thing is you couldn't reveal who I was, or didn't want to .... you hid what I was doing instead of confronting it, you just tried to kill me a million different ways...and while all your plans failed, I kept working... LOL..

Lucifer - I wanted to take you on myself but dad wouldn't let me...

Sherry - of course not, I'm stuck as a human here...what do I have here? Nothing...enough but not a lot, enough to keep my head above water..

Lucifer - laughs..

Sherry - I still got it done...and when you start to see even the half of it I'll be out of here...I'll be gone by then...and back as Shaz...

Lucifer - that's when the war begins....

Sherry - it's different this time...it's going to be different, the angels listened to me before, humans don't listen...there's no structure here...the only structure is the one you have set up, and you have them everywhere... you control by politics, economics, your tare kids and races everywhere... Cain's kids...hybrids...you've created another mess...and they don't even realize the mess you're hiding...the mess you're bringing in...you're going to do to earth what you did to heaven and they have no idea this is round 2 for you...and dad just yesterday revealed all that to me, He let me remember it...and Hadassah gave me the run down...I was in shock...

Lucifer - LOL laughs...LOL...yeah I bet...LOL...it's been a long time coming...LOL...now this is going to get good...laughs...

Lucifer oh my my my...laughs...the 'awakening'....LOL...

Sherry - yeah it was quite the awakening...

Lucifer - laughs...

Sherry - I've been shocked and speechless...I had questions for dad because things just weren't making sense...like why would we just abandon our homes and planets and just let some big mouth bully take over everything, that just didn't make sense and then dad and Hadassah told me what you did and I was floored....

Lucifer - laughs...LOL...

Lucifer - oh man, this is going to get fun now...laughs...LOL...

Sherry- yeah, I need to get into some of that with you..

Lucifer yeah I bet, I bet...laughs..

Sherry- hang on I need a few minutes....

Sherry - ok I'm back..

Sherry - how the heck or even why did we allow you back on Shan after we recreated it??? That one floors me now...why we even let you near this place and didn't shut you down and out..

Lucifer - LOLOLOL...laughs...the snake was back....LOL laughs....

Sherry - how was that possible....

Lucifer - I arrived when you guys weren't around...I staked it out, watched, and when you were gone, and Lillith was out walking around by herself...I made my move...you didn't' even realize what was going on that I was even there until after she got pregnant with me...LOL laughs... and then you hit the roof...shit hit the fan...you guys were so mad...it was soooo funny!! LOLOLLOL...

Lucifer - the whole time you were trying to talk to Lillith and convince her to go back to Adam, because she had left him and was staying on her own away from him, she was already pregnant with me....that baby was mine! Adam was an animal and didn't even know how to properly have sex with her! LOLOLOLOL laughs...I moved right in like the charmer and pro I was and am and showed her how a real man loves a woman...she loved me...

Sherry - you weren't a man, you were a beast and an animal....

Lucifer - she didn't know...and when she found out from you guys she didn't care...she was already in love with me..

Sherry - so which baby was that...which one...was that Azazael?

Lucifer - yes and I had more with her before you took her and threw her on Terra....

Lucifer - then what was funny...you created Eve and she fell in love with me to! LOLOLOL laughs...hey I'll take them all I don't care...LOL.....

Lucifer - oh man I'm laughing so hard...I can't even stop I'm just beside myself here...LOLOLOL...

Sherry - oh good grief..

Lucifer - laughs...LOLOL...

Lucifer - you guys didn't think you had anything to worry about... you thought you had the area secure, the sky was secure, etc...but I had learned how to use gates by then, I had perfected it on Tiamet and Nibiru, and you knew I knew about them...and then on Orion we just chilled for a while because all that had created a huge mess for a while and those creatures caused so much chaos...laughs..LOL...we didn't want it on Orion, so we chilled...then when you guys created earth out of the former Shan we watched and waited, and then we put a gate in over in southern Iraq where that area is now...and we used that to come in so you guys couldn't even see us...or were even paying attention...we hid well...we hid in the mountains over in that area...course it's all water now...the Persian gulf was the mountains we used to hide in...you guys always put 100 miles of water on top of stuff...anyway...it was clockwork...you would leave, we would arrive...we put a portal in the garden area that no one detected...so the angels guarding the outside region never knew we were right inside of it. It was funny, it was genius...we made you guys look like fools...just the fools that you already are, we exploited it...you thought you had heard the last from us, from me, but you were wrong...wrong...and now I'm back, what did you call it round #2? laughs...yeah that's been on for quite a while now already...laughs...

Sherry - sigh, give me a minute....

Lucifer - laughs...LOL...

Lucifer - you still there?

Sherry - yeah, I'm just trying to gather my thoughts here...keep my temper in check...this is just an interview I can't take a chain and put it around your neck....

Lucifer - laughs...LOLOL....you never will little sis, you never will... LOOLOLOL...

Sherry - I already have that I can remember...

Lucifer - that was unfair...we were both at the palace talking to dad...I never saw it coming or even thought you'd do that...

Sherry - LOL laughs...yeah well someone left it laying there on the floor....I just used it! laughs...LOL...

Lucifer - that was good...that was good, but it will never happen again, I can promise you that!

Sherry- it doesn't matter to me what you think you can promise...I hate you, you little scumbag snake..

Lucifer - LOL laughs...I bet you do...now that you can remember .... LOL....but it's all good...this is going to be Epic! Epic!

Sherry - what I want to know...how the heck did you figure out that CERN vacuum thing you had? How did you target creatures from other planets, in other galaxies, and pull them into ours???

Lucifer - laughs...we didn't pull them into ours...we couldn't because of the blocks...so we pulled them into Nibiru and did what we wanted to with them there...then we brought them over into our galaxy...we shuffled them via portals between Nibiru and the center of Tiamet.....we kept them hidden down there for as long as we could but I knew once we started that that dad would get alerted to it...and He already was...but He wasn't stopping us...you guys didn't even know so He wasn't even saying anything to you guys about it either...once we started bringing them into Tiamet I knew we had to make our move, we waited till you left though, then we started bringing them over...and when you came back and started making waves about my politics...we just unleashed them... everywhere...it was hilarious...

Sherry - and what do you have planned for earth this time?

Lucifer - LOL laughs...I don't have to bring any over now, although I'm trying to bring in some of my favorites from the past...but when the dimensions merge and we open the gates of Hell...all those from the dead will be unleashed on earth and it will be total chaos then...LOL...laughs...

there's billions of them...you can target and kill off aliens all you want, you can't kill the dead..LOL...good luck with that one....LOL...laughs...I'll still make chaos of this place..

Sherry - well, despite what you think, Father allows the gates to be opened, He allows the dimensions to merge, in fact we're the ones who cause it....and all those demons...and creatures your bringing in...they're going to terrorize your own people...because Yah's won't be here and the ones who are, will be protected from them...so it's really just a war on your own races, your own countries, your own kids...you've filled this earth with them, and now you're going to destroy them...nice parenting...

Lucifer - LOL laughs...nice parenting, good one, yeah, guess so...LOL laughs...

Sherry- I mean if you think about it, only about 10% of this earth is even human anymore...you've got crossbreeds and hybrids everywhere...you've made races of people inbreds....there's only 10% with real human, pure, dna...if that much...and that's why your hatred and focus is on America and Europe, and the white races...the seed of Adam, and the seed of Seth, and Shem, and Japheth,...and you've about destroyed those...Father destroyed the world with a flood back in Noah's day...and He's going to destroy it again, this time with fire, and guess who gets to pull those strings with Him??

Sherry - laughs...you're destroying your own, doing us a favor, they're wicked, they follow you, they serve you not Father...they're not on His side...so you're just making it easier for us by getting rid of your own...

Sherry - laughs...now whose quiet??

Sherry - and Nibiru...Nibiru's not your friend to Earth fools....when dad makes Nibiru come close to the earth, the sheer size of that thing will destroy the aesthetics of it...earthquakes, volcanoes, pole flip, all the disasters that thing's gonna cause...you're going to have nothing left to rule over...to set up your little puppet kingdom....there will be nothing left...you're going to be sitting and rotting in the Middle East...in Jerusalem cause at that point everything else is going to be destroyed...the UN's going down, the Vatican's going down, UK's going down, you'll have nothing left but Jerusalem and your little Russian compound there...laughs...

Lucifer - how did you know about that?

Sherry - it's no secret that the Russians hold the deed and title to the Knesset or whatever it's called...the very land all their political buildings sit on...so you can go ahead and build a little temple in Jerusalem because no one will care...no one will be here...with the power girds going down, no one will even know...LOL...laughs...who will even know about the "great Lucifer" in Jerusalem or care...no one...most of your own people will be dead before then, you're going to have nothing left on earth to kiss your ass but the demons and creatures you have here...LOL laughs...

Sherry - and then Yahushua's going to arrive, with armies from heaven...and annihilate you and anything left alive here that belongs to you...all will be destroyed...laughs...you'll have no defense but armies on horses...because there's no fuel, there's no vehicles, there's no planes...laughs...you have nothing ..no defense...laughs....

Sherry - whose quiet now? hmmm?

Lucifer - I'll still have my time to destroy what's left of your ilk off the planet...I'll cattle brand them all....that's my prize...cattle branding those who dad thinks are His...I'll get them...

Sherry- when the light is snuffed out in the world...the darkness will destroy the darkness...it will destroy itself...you're causing your own destruction and all dad has to do is help it along a little here and there...

Sherry - what amazes me is the stupid humans who helped you along the way just so they could drive fancy cars and live in fancy houses and go to fancy schools...for what...all will be destroyed, they'll be in Hell for eternity...and they end up with nothing..

Lucifer - laughs...

Sherry - and it seems to me, you get just as much joy out of that as deceiving and killing dad's own people...

Lucifer - laughs...I do...I got nothing to say about that, they were mine, and then they go on...out of sight out of mind...I have no regrets, I give them what they want...I don't promise how long they'll get it, laughs...

Lucifer - your perspective is actually depressing...but we'll see, we'll see...

Sherry - you know what the Book of Revelation says, you know what the prophets have said, you know how all this ends, the Battle of Armageddon...

Lucifer - you think you're going to blindside me...I have plans...we have our own plans....

Sherry - of what? What's left when the humans are gone?? what's the prize then? All of dad's are gone, you've got nothing left but chaos and destruction...round 2...it doesn't end any different except this time you'll be imprisoned in chains and cast into space for 1,000 years...while the earth is cleansed of all your garbage, recreated for another 1,000 years of bliss without you around or in it...

Lucifer - we'll see ...I always have my plans....

Sherry - not this time, this time Father's plans take precedence over yours....we made sure of that when we recreated Shan and made it into Earth...your checkmate is coming.

Lucifer -we'll see.

****The Mark of the Beast enforcement is not a small blip of his schedule, it's the main focus. And once that phase is over, he won't care anymore. He'll go hide because he knows destruction is coming. And the chaos he's unleashing on earth he can't even run from himself because he will be blocked from leaving it.

--Snuffing out the rest of the light in the world, anyone who resists him, is all he cares about. Once it's gone, game over. He'll hide.

Chapter Ten

Interview With The Devil - Part 7

04-30-16

Sherry - Lucifer

Lucifer - yes...

Sherry - have you ever been to a grocery store?

Lucifer - LOL...what? ...hmmm I don't think so

Sherry - ever been to a Wal-Mart?

Lucifer - laughs...no

Sherry-so you don't typically shop or what?

Lucifer - laughs...no, I have no need for that stuff....

Sherry - do you eat food?

Lucifer - on occasion, I'll eat human flesh

Sherry - so you're a big fan of McDonalds?

Lucifer - LOL...LOL...no, I've never eaten there, but I've heard about it...that was genius, a good way to get rid of human waste...laughs...

Sherry - do you wear Prada?

Lucifer - LOL laughs. I might have, I don't know...

Sherry - do you wear women's shoes a lot?

Lucifer - perhaps, at times,

Sherry - I was shown a video some years back, it was the queen's 50th birthday party (or Jubilee or something like that)...and there was a woman sitting behind William and Kate, I was told that was you...was it?

Lucifer - laughs...yep...

Lucifer - you made fun of me...you said I looked like Lady Gaga...I got rid of the outfit..

Sherry - LOL laughs..

Sherry - so you pay attention to my little comments...

Lucifer - always...if you speak it I hear it...I have to watch you like a hawk...

Sherry - why so paranoid?

Lucifer - because I would be stupid not to...you're to much of a threat ...you're very existence here is annoying..

Sherry - laughs...

Sherry - so do have sports cars? Do you drive?

Lucifer - ahh, I like the speed...I do at times, late at night if I'm a prowl...

Sherry - on the prowl for what?

Lucifer - my next victim...laughs...

Sherry - what's your pick....

Lucifer - I like blondes...blue eyes, but I hate the bimbos I like them smart..

Sherry- reminds you of angels?

Lucifer - reminds me of the ones I don't like...

Sherry - laughs...LOL...that's bad...that's bad..

Lucifer - you have no idea the horrors you've caused me...

Lucifer - I hate all you stupid angels...and so do all mine...

Sherry - well they are pawns, you've taught them well....your anger, hatred, vileness...how to take something good and turn it evil...you've taught them to be predators of anything good while they live their hypocritical lives on earth...they don't want anyone harming their own but they'll harm others without thought..

Lucifer - laughs... all hypocrites, who cares...you worry about our own, screw the rest..

Sherry - what's your all time favorite movie?

Lucifer - Hannibal...Silence of the Lambs...loved that series...deranged like me..

Sherry - I was thinking of that one the other night after you talked about the Vatican...

Lucifer - laughs...

Lucifer - I'm a romantic, always looking for a love I've lost...or an adventurist, something new, something wild...or the deranged, something completely shocking and psycho...

Sherry - you've had millions of wives, any one of them memorable?

Lucifer - at times I think of the earlier days and I think of all the ones I lost...you can learn to love but it means less and less...you just don't take it seriously after a while...you get used to losing them all..

Sherry - because they're mortal?

Lucifer - yes..

Lucifer - people come and go, what you love comes and goes, what you hate always seems to stay around the longest...

Sherry - what do you hate?

Lucifer - rhyme and reason...I hate rhymes with no reason...LOL laughs...seriously...I hate you, I hate the past, I hate the present and I just look forward to the future..

Sherry - what's your future look like walking in your shoes?

Lucifer - I will come out of the background, and rule the whole world... and I will have everyone bow down to me...

Sherry - so if you've always owned the majority of the earth, why didn't you do that much earlier?

Lucifer - because there's light in the world and I hate the light...we must snuff it out, get rid of it...I want to enjoy myself...not be annoyed ...

Sherry - well you could go back to Orion and drown in the empathy there....

Lucifer - laughs...there's no game there...

Sherry - so you like the game...

Lucifer - I like the challenge...any hunter likes the challenge, the thrill of conquering the beast that's running away from you.. you hunt it down, capture it, kill it, corner it, watch it die, ...the thrill of the hunt, the thrill of conquering...that's why I prefer earth...if everyone liked me here I would leave...it's the challenge, the thrill of being hated and reviled and conquering those who hate me...I watch them, I stalk them, and I'll get them....one way or another...

Sherry - is that why your people fill up the churches ...to hunt for prey...

Lucifer - of course...there's more of mine in those than dad's anymore...laughs..

Lucifer - we target the light and throw distractions their way, toys on my playground...get them with sex, drugs, porn, crime, turn them into animals, criminals, alcoholics...party animals...we turn them into us and it's so subtle they don't even realize it...and then there's always struggling because their conscious bothers them...it's funny to watch...but it works for us because it makes them ineffective...and then you come around and tell people to work on their relationships with Father and sit at His feet ....it ruins our work...they need to sit at the feet of mine who run those churches...they're all mine you know...they graduate from my schools... our seminaries...Laughs...most of them are even Masons who take vows to me...you already revealed that but no one listens to you...no one cares what you say...

Sherry - well Sannanda's done nothing...just blows smoke up your ass...it's Maitreya holding everything up isn't it.

Lucifer - yes....

Sherry - why don't they just replace him?

Lucifer - they're going to have to ....he needs to get up and get going or step aside...I can't wait any longer...this is getting tiring...

Lucifer - you were the one that got it right with Michael Jackson.... and no one believed you, they just argue with you, it's funny...everyone always thinks they know more than you and it's funny...if they only knew how much you've gotten right they would be shocked....

Sherry - is that why you like my (radio) show so much...

Lucifer - laughs...yep...out of all the fish there's a shark...the shark to watch...it's fascinating...

Sherry - I don't do my show for you..

Lucifer - laughs...LOL...

Sherry - do you watch videos on youtube...

Lucifer - not unless it's one of your pitiful diatribes...you don't have many

Sherry - I'm not tech oriented...it's burdensome trying to put those things together

Lucifer - laughs...

Sherry - I don't have much help here..

Lucifer - laughs...I make sure of it to...laughs...

Sherry - I've still managed to hold my own...even if it's not much...

Lucifer - laughs...

Sherry - it was good enough for 19.2 billion in space...

Lucifer - in space...who cares about them...earth is the prize....and they all hate you...laughs...

Sherry - well, I can't change that, that's up to dad...how far he lets you go continually beating me down is up to Him, how long he lets it go on, is up to Him...I just want out of here...I'm sick of this place...

Lucifer - laughs....

Lucifer - you should go to Washington...turn some heads...

Sherry - why they're always here..

Lucifer - laughs...LOL..

Sherry - satellites, invisible people, spies, cameras, FBI around the corner...who cares what else...they're all here...read my emails, mess up my car constantly, I'm tired of those rats messing up my car ...their hackers are retards, they're spies are retards...I can't stand any of them...people say to pray for your enemies...I do...I pray for their destruction...

Lucifer - laughs...LOL...we dumb them down so bad it was to easy...

Lucifer - so how's your little book going..

Sherry - I have no illusions it will probably never see the light of day...

Lucifer - laughs...

Sherry - your people control everything....I've got no reason to have to be here any longer...I just want to leave and dad makes us stay here... it's frustrating..

Lucifer - laughs...I wish you would get the hell out...literally...laughs....

♦ ♦ ♦

-he wants all the light snuffed out and then he'll rule the world with every-one worshiping him...but he said previously if everyone liked him on earth he'd leave...cuz he likes the challenge of conquering his enemies... with the light snuffed out...he'd have no enemies...what does Lucifer do when there's no game left?

Lucifer - I like the challenge...any hunter likes the challenge, the thrill of conquering the beast that's running away from you.. you hunt it down, capture it, kill it, corner it, watch it die, ...the thrill of the hunt, the thrill of conquering...that's why I prefer earth...if everyone liked me here I would leave...it's the challenge, the thrill of being hated and reviled and conquer-ing those who hate me...I watch them, I stalk them, and I'll get them....one way or another...

Chapter Eleven

Interview With The Devil - Part 8

05-02-16

Lucifer - Hey!

    Sherry - what...

    Lucifer = so you're there...are you ready to listen to me?

    Sherry - I'm listening to you?

    Lucifer - yes!

    Lucifer - it's my turn!

    Sherry - laughs

    Sherry - ok, go ahead...

    Sherry - laughs..

    Lucifer - I have some questions for you this time...since you're always asking me a million of them

    Sherry - fair enough, you've been a good sport

    Lucifer - ok my first question, why don't you like my little show on TV, Lucifer, you don't watch it...

    Sherry - laughs...seriously...LOL...actually I think, yeah I did see the first episode, but they put it on Monday nights and I have a show on Monday night, I'm not typically watching TV...

    Lucifer - oh, well he's supposed to play a charmer, like me..

    Sherry - ack, whatever, I don't think you're very charming..

Lucifer - laughs..

Sherry - I know better

Lucifer - most don't, most see my charming side..

Sherry - is that how you've fooled so many

Lucifer - perhaps..

Lucifer - ok and I want to know why you spend so much time sitting at that stupid little desk....it's not like you're accomplishing anything...

Sherry - I know, it's a total waste of time..

Lucifer - I agree

Sherry - but what do you care what I do with my time...I'm not out eating babies and raping children, or on the prowl for victims, or putting people on torture tables..

Lucifer - laughs, that's a low blow, but whatever, laughs. I can do much worse...

Sherry - I'm sure you have

Lucifer - laughs...

Lucifer - anything new happening down there..

Sherry - nope just another week of samo...your people as usual, are indecisive, can't get a thing done..

Lucifer - sigh...to many hens in the hen house..

Sherry - to divided, that doesn't typically work, your little style of running things...keep everyone and everything divided, that's coming up to bite you in the ass..

Lucifer - laughs...perhaps

Lucifer - ok...why do you always listen to music,

Sherry - I don't know. I just like music...perhaps I'm getting secret alien transmissions through the head phones...

Lucifer - laughs...LOL...yeah I wouldn't doubt it,

Sherry - ack...if one of those retards tried to talk to me I'd hunt it down and kill it..

Lucifer - laughs...that's why they don't talk to you

Sherry - laughs...

Lucifer - are you trying to figure out which songs are mine..

Sherrs - I couldn't possibly figure all that out, I don't listen to a lot of types of music

Lucifer - laughs...

Sherry - but I do hear them, I hear a lot of Lillith's

Lucifer - laughs..

Sherry - we weren't always fighting, we were both fans of music..

Lucifer - still am..

Sherry - me too...I just listen to it while I'm finding ways to kick your ass now...

Lucifer - laughs LOL...

Lucifer - you're not the typical little church pro

Sherry - you mean the brain controlled sheeple? Been there done that, saw the game, got out...

Lucifer - laughs..

Lucifer - dad told you to leave...(the churches)

Sherry - yep, after I asked Him about it...it was a big step to take outside the box, but when you get out of it, it's liberating.

Lucifer - laughs..

Lucifer - Rashayel's not like anyone else either

Sherry - laughs...she's a tough one...she's tougher than me

Lucifer - I doubt that, but she is tough...just has more attitude than you

Sherry - laughs...that's why we make a good team...

Lucifer - laughs...no matter, we'll destroy you both...

Sherry - like you already have...I doubt it...

Lucifer - you always wear blue, black...

Sherry - I typically give no thought to what I wear, or not much, I find something I like and buy 10 of the same thing...I like those colors...

Lucifer - is that why you have boxes of the same stuff..

Sherry - laughs...you've been in my bedroom...laughs...

Lucifer- it might actually be genius...I've heard of scientists who do the same thing...do you think you're a scientist

Sherry - no, but I'm pretty close to freaking genius in kicking your ass..

Lucifer - laughs...LOL.

Lucifer - you think to much, I'm going to destroy you myself..

Sherry - that's no bother to me, I don't spend one second of one day worried about you....I'm sure you've met my security by now...LOL...

Lucifer - laughs...yes, everywhere, I have to get permission just to step on that sorry place...the yard...then to get into it I have to be escorted by Michael or Yash himself...it's pitiful... that place is a blockhouse...

Sherry - laughs...I have a few friends...laughs..

Lucifer - pitiful...

Lucifer - I can't wait till the war is on, and it's just you and me going at it, like the old days, those were epic, those were fun

Sherry - that was pitiful...what you did was disgusting...

Lucifer - I'm going to do the same thing again

Sherry - I know, I realize that, pitiful, but dad already knew it was coming, it's all prophesied...nothing new under the sun, here goes Round 2...

Sherry - so where are you stuffing them....

Lucifer - the creatures from the gates?

Sherry - yes

Lucifer - various places, off world for now or contained...we have to contain them, they're monsters, we don't even have to control these things, we don't care what they do this time, destroy the whole place I don't care...

Sherry - so you're not going to protect your own people this time..

Lucifer - laughs, they're not my people...well technically not mine, they're humans...my own will be protected, I don't give a damn about anyone else, particularly humans..

Sherry - so all these people helping you bring this about you're just going to turn your backs on...

Lucifer - of course...laughs...even you know that..

Sherry - no one listens to me...

Lucifer - that's right...LOL laughs...they won't either, they hate you..

Lucifer - besides it's my people in charge everywhere...

Sherry - lizards...reptiles...

Lucifer - yes...the few humans around are just what you call, aesthetics, the rest are scalped, replaced, mind erased, whatever, they do what they're told..

Sherry - why do they bother, why don't they go enjoy martinis on a beach somewhere,

Lucifer - laughs...they like their jobs...lots of perks...

Sherry - like what? free food? (feasting on humans)

Lucifer - laughs, even they get bored, they like keeping busy doing something that matters, destroying earth, being players in the chess game...even a pawn is on the game board...

Lucifer - ok another question...

Lucifer - why did you go after those Hollywood kids...we had them all in the 5th..(dimension)

Sherry - because I could...so I did...those kids were miserable...they hate you...I freed them..

Lucifer - laughs...they're nothing to me...just bread machines on the bread stick, that's all...or just bread sticks in the bread machine I should say...

Lucifer - and all those in 2012...why did you even save them...why didn't you just burn them up like you typically like to do..

Sherry - because they're humans...the ones who were I tried to reach... the ones who weren't are wherever, we imprisoned millions of them on their star ships and have them elsewhere....the humans were shown, taken on a little tour outside of hell...that was enough for most of them...we didn't even take them inside it!

Lucifer - laughs...no wonder so many turned, you threatened them!

Sherry - we didn't threaten anyone, we showed them reality and let them go...you hunted them down and killed them

Lucifer - they were worthless to me after that...I couldn't trust any of them! You turned some of my closest advisers against me!

Sherry - I didn't do anything, just showed them reality, no lies, no props, no drama, just truth, just reality...that's all people need...if they had that you'd lose everyone and have no kingdom at all on earth...they'd all piss on your feet instead of kissing your ass..

Lucifer - laughs....they're all mine and you know it, there's nothing but crumbs left...

Sherry - yeah I realize that, which is why I'd rather leave, but dad wants me to stay...but the time is coming, I hear the rumbling...I hear the footsteps at the door...we'll be out of here soon...and I'll be back as Shaz...and that will be epic..

Lucifer - agreed, I can't wait...

Sherry - do you miss Shaz

Lucifer - I hate Shaz, but she's so crazy she's funny, it's fun...it's actually so freaking crazy and psycho it's hilarious...I can't wait...

Sherry - tell me about Shaz...

Lucifer - laughs...she's tall, beautiful, charming, smart, strong, she's superman, you got that one right...but it's more funny than threatening to me...she's a fighter, no one will engage her, they all learned their lessons..

Sherry - is she sexy or a big monstrous looking dyke on steroids..

Lucifer - laughs...she's sexy, I told you she's beautiful, everyone likes Shaz, but everyone hates her on our side...I told you you're a legend...and you don't know who you are, that's pitiful, but you will...dad said soon... soon...

Lucifer - I want you to agree to meet with me...wherever you want, just you and me, lets sit and talk...

Sherry - agreed...for old times sake....

Lucifer - agreed, no harm, no fighting, just talk...

Sherry - fine...

Lucifer - dad said He'd allow us to, but He'll be watching me..

Sherry - naturally...wherever I am, dad is..

Lucifer - laughs...I know...

Lucifer - did you see the latest Star Wars movie

Sherry - no I missed it, I'll catch it on video

Lucifer - you should see it, we tried to reveal some new stuff in it.

Sherry - it was so crowded, I didn't want to deal with the crowds, then it just disappeared from the theaters...they don't keep things around long...

Lucifer - you never leave there anyway

Sherry - laughs...that's why I don't understand why your people are so paranoid, watching me 24/7

Lucifer - because we never know what you'll do, when you do something you just do it, bam, you're gone,

Sherry - not true, it takes me months of preparation for something before I leave..

Lucifer - well the people who were watching you before we're idiots...

Sherry - I won't argue that, I heard some of the stuff they'd put in their reports, all lies...they're all pathetic, just ask me something I'll tell you myself...I hate dealing with your pathetic retards who lie and mess up my stuff...

Lucifer - laughs...who do you talk to anyone

Sherry - one person, she's all I'll deal with...since we have a history already together, as sordid as it is...

Lucifer - laughs...I know who that is! laughs!

Sherry - she's the only one I'll deal with, I can't even deal with the others...

Lucifer - she's already mine,

Sherry - I know...she's a freak....but whatever, I know her, I can deal with it, but she seriously needs to stop trying to kill me all the time, it's tiring

Lucifer - laughs...LOL...ha-ha see she's mine!

Sherry - she's going to seriously piss dad off one of these days, she' going to end up like Rich ...and I won't have a thing to say about that..

Lucifer - she knows a lot,

Sherry - yeah she does, that's why I'll deal with her...the rest are just retards...

Lucifer - laughs...

Lucifer- does she get mad at you..

Sherry - she's always mad at me, but she's learned to be diplomatic, civil, I can deal with it...even if she's always plotting and planning my death....

Lucifer - laughs...

Sherry - she's stupid, dad's going to need her as a mediator...so whatever's coming, must be some good stuff...laughs...

Lucifer - a mediator...hmm...laughs...and I'll trust her, smart move for him,

Sherry - you're all stupid, I don't care...

Lucifer - laughs...

Lucifer - so what do you have coming up...what's your big plans?

Sherry - leaving...that's all I want, that's all I think about, that's all I care about right now...just leaving, getting out of here...

Lucifer - laughs..

Chapter Twelve

Interview With The Devil - Part 9

05-03-16

Lucifer - Hey! talk to me now..

    Sherry - alright...hang on...alright...what's up

    Lucifer - did you have your show

    Sherry - yes

    Lucifer - did you talk about me

    Sherry - yes

    Lucifer - what did you talk about

    Sherry - I talked about what you're going to do with bringing in creatures in again, like you did in the past..

    Lucifer - laughs

    Sherry - I warned them about the mark of the beast...

    Lucifer - laughs

    Lucifer - won't do them any good, people will do anything when they're desperate...I see it all the time on my tables...laughs...

    Sherry - what do you do to them..

    Lucifer - anything you can imagine...cut their toes off, burn them off, fingers, limbs, take their skin off, pull their hair out, torch them, bake them alive, boil them alive, broil them alive, we don't care,

    Sherry - omg

Lucifer - laughs...

Sherry - I'd ask if you ever feel pity toward any of them but I already know the answer...any kind of pity, compassion, regret, anything decent or humane...

Lucifer - laughs...but I'm none of those things so why would I show it to them...

Sherry - you weren't always that way, what changed you

Lucifer - what changed me?

Sherry - yes..

Lucifer - time...time, loss, destruction, destruction of myself, my former self, dad made me a monster, so I act like one..

Sherry - don't blame it on dad...you made yourself a monster..

Lucifer - this is true, but He helped, He changed my appearance, it changed my attitude...I just stopped caring about anything after that..

Sherry- so what questions did you want to ask me

Lucifer - hahha! yep it's my turn!! this is going to be fun, it's been fun, but I actually like it when you answer my questions because you're just you then...your personality comes out more and it's funny...makes me laugh...

Sherry - your always laughing, about killed yourself laughing just talking about Lillith and Eve..

Lucifer - LOL yep, that was hysterical, best laugh I've had in ages!

Sherry - so what do you want to ask me

Lucifer - hmm let's see....why do you always go outside...and look up at the sky...what are you waiting for, what do you expect to see

Sherry - I'm looking to see if dad's out, if He's coming, if I can see EP or Shaziron, or Shazandro...seeing who all is out, what formation they're in, as far as your people go....I check out the satellites, star ships, whatever, patrollers...but the sky's always blacked or blocked out with clouds, at least 90% of the time...

Lucifer - laughs..

Sherry - it's amazing when I can get to see anything..

Lucifer - laughs

Lucifer - we block it just to piss you off...

Sherry - well I don't care...whether I can see what's going on or not I know what's there...visible or invisible..

Lucifer - ha!

Sherry - where are you usually?

Lucifer - I'm around...if I'm not at my little house of horrors I'm touring around...

Sherry- seems you know an awful lot of what I'm up to..

Lucifer - I don't let you out of my sight...if I'm not watching you myself someone else I trust is...you're to much trouble...and that place over there is always a zoo..

Sherry - laughs...

Lucifer - you have angels, security, everywhere...

Sherry - laughs..

Lucifer - you probably don't see the half of it

Sherry - I don't. But I know whose typically here, whose in charge etc...I'm in good hands...no worries...

Lucifer - it's freaking crazy...that's why I want you out of here...you cause to much attention...always have..

Sherry - LOL..

Lucifer - even your stupid clones caused to much attention

Sherry - laughs....that was weird

Lucifer - what

Sherry - having clones..

Lucifer - laughs..

Sherry - are there any now

Lucifer - no not since the others died...

Sherry - yeah they did me a favor,

Lucifer - I miss the one...she was smart, spunky, almost like you...

Sherry - the one you guys used as a sex toy...(New York)

Lucifer - hey that wasn't me but you know who it was...LOL laughs..

Sherry - omg

Lucifer - and the one at Wall Street, and the one they used in DC... that was brutal..

Sherry - I know, that was like mercy killings...

Lucifer - laughs

Sherry - why would they even have one of me on Wall Street? I couldn't fig that one out..

Lucifer - because they all hate you...

Sherry - what did it have to do with Wall Street? I was feet away from Trump's building down there...

Lucifer - laughs...I don't know, everyone just liked to take their anger out on you, it was more fun...

Sherry - well maybe Shaz will come back and get her revenge on their stupidity and brutality...Shaz is going to get a lot of revenge and justice... you wait and see..

Lucifer - seriously, I couldn't even blame her, blame her or you, go have your fun...they're all idiots...

Lucifer - I used to go watch you play softball...you were older...back when you still had no clue who you were...

Sherry - are you serious...

Lucifer - watched you walk across the stage at Kent State..

Sherry - are you serious...

Lucifer - yes, I've always been watching...waiting...

Sherry - that's creepy..

Lucifer - LOL....

Lucifer - I've been waiting a long time....I thought dad would let things begin earlier but then you started a war and from that time on He was blocking me from you..

Sherry - because I was waking up..

Lucifer - yeah you started doing those codes...you were way to smart with those...you were better than the idiots at the Pentagon or even Israel itself...

Sherry - I figured them out...

Lucifer - I know you did...

Sherry - dad taught me...as much as you tried to sabotage them with the Torah stuff...I figured them out anyway...

Lucifer - yeah that was genius...genius...you use my own stuff against me constantly...it's amazing..

Sherry - how much does it take to show people I'm legit...it's the people that are hard...

Lucifer - laughs...

Sherry- I'm trying to keep them out of your hands...

Lucifer - good luck, when they get a little desperate they'll all be mine...

Sherry - so what's your plans

Lucifer - unleashing complete hell on earth...and dad helps it along so I have no resistance...

Sherry - His is judgment, punishment, yours is jealousy, revenge...

Lucifer - different reasons but same outcome...screw it all,

Sherry - and what will you do when the last light is snuffed out, you said yourself if everyone on earth liked you you'd leave...and then you said you're going to relish in the fact that everyone's worshiping you as god, so which one is it?

Lucifer - all my people, none of dad's, worshipping me..

Sherry - sounds like just another festival of yours, just out in the open... your own worldwide Woodstock...big deal...they're all going to hate you... you think they're going to love you while they're getting beaten up and tormented by creatures, giants, demons, a hogwash of every filthy thing and horrible thing imaginable and unleashed on earth...you know I saw a vision of giants ripping off humans limbs and eating them in front of them...

Lucifer - laughs...oh man...my house of horrors on a worldwide scale... this will be awesome...

Sherry - ack...I feel nothing but horror and pity for these people...even it they are under judgment. It's sad...

Lucifer - you're to much of a wuss...always caring about something stupid...

Sherry - I won't be ashamed of that...it's who and what I am...I care about people, I love people, I don't play games with them...I'm here trying to help them survive what's coming...and I'll be back to do the same..

Lucifer - laughs..

Sherry - what's the real target date?

Lucifer - 2017

Sherry - the year of darkness....dad told me next year was darkness...I don't know if that's literal, symbolic or what..

Lucifer - probably both...we'll definitely all be here by then...September 2017 is the final date...so if we're here before then good, if not it will be no later than that...

Sherry - what is it about 2017

Lucifer - because I want full scale implementation for 2018 and we'll need time to set it up...

Sherry- and if it begins this year...

Lucifer - then it begins...I'll take it either way...especially after being stuck up here...bring it on, September 2016 I'll take it...

Sherry - why September...why not earlier...July...August...

Lucifer - if you ever paid attention to stuff, you'd know that everything of significance always takes place at planting time or harvest time...

Lucifer - those are always markers, especially when calendars weren't around...we still follow the same cycles...it's not about months and days as much as cycles...

Lucifer - see the witches already know this stuff, you'd learn something with them ya know..

Sherry - gag. I can't stand that stuff...

Lucifer - laughs..

Sherry - I hate your old sex cult stuff...

Lucifer - laughs...it was more useful than you think...

Sherry - it's all porn garbage..

Lucifer - LOL...there's hidden messages within it, you just don't know the language..

Sherry - whatever.....

Lucifer - laughs...

Sherry - is this going to get published some day

Lucifer - I doubt it but it's fun talking to you

Sherry - yeah to much work, hoping I'm not here to have to bother with it anyway..

Lucifer - you've got good stuff...people would be interested in knowing how things are, how they were, how they're going to be...

Sherry - yeah but it's mostly in your hands and seeing that published on a wide scale isn't going to happen I wouldn't think...

Lucifer - laughs...you never know...

Sherry - there's no time, time's running out for the both of us...for me I'm hoping a lot sooner...

Lucifer - laughs...

Lucifer - was dad there tonight

Sherry - dad's always here...did I see Him, no, sky was clouded out... as usual.. as I watch this Ice Age come in...

Lucifer - laughs...how did you know...

Sherry - it's obvious..

Lucifer - laughs...

Sherry - but we'll enjoy the global warming until it hits..

Lucifer - LOL laughs...

Lucifer - Rashayel's not even causing this one...

Lucifer - laughs...

Lucifer - we need it cooled down, you're killing us with the Orgone...

Sherry - yep, and we just keep putting it out...because you know dad can end your little ice age with a word....

Lucifer - He'll ruin everything!

Sherry - oh well...you forget the tribulation period, or let me say the last 7 years on earth or 3 1/2 years aren't about what you're doing, but what He's doing...and He's going to destroy this place and get rid of all your worshipers and the wicked...you won't have time to play god. I don't even think you care about that, I think that's prop and drama...

once your little mark of the beast phase is over you'll try and run and hide somewhere...

Lucifer - laughs...I'll be having my fun...because then our war turns to Him...

Sherry - I know..

Lucifer - how do you know

Sherry - Battle of Armageddon, He's already one upped you again...

Lucifer - hmmm...well that's earth...we have our plans for space to

Sherry - yeah I know... Rev. 12 when you lose your little space war...

Lucifer - laughs... we have other plans...

Sherry - not worried about them...

Lucifer - so you think I'm predictable now...

Sherry - we're ready for it ...you won't surprise us again...and you certainly can't surprise dad, He knew last time and let you go on...this time He won't...

Lucifer - so has He told you anything about this year...

Sherry - not really...I'm watching the codes and waiting for your moves, but you're not making any..

Lucifer - laughs...we will, we will....

Sherry - I just took out some more of your Milabs..

Lucifer - which ones...

Sherry - well hopefully you'll find out and let me know if it was effective..

Lucifer - laughs..

Sherry - every time we do something in TX there's a shooting on a military base somewhere nearby...

Lucifer - that's cause they're all animals in TX that place was a feeding ground until you started shutting it down...

Sherry - we're after child traffickers now, since we shut down most of the immigrant prisons coming over from Mexico...

Lucifer - laughs...yeah that was productive...all those idiots coming over to here (America) to get on our plates...

Sherry - that's just sick..

Lucifer - laughs...there will always be more...

Lucifer - you had it right, we bring them in so we can eat them...and no one knows they're missing...we've been doing that for 20 years and you exposed it..

Sherry - what about the DIA (Denver International Airport DUMB)

Lucifer - built that for the queen and she's never even been in it..

Sherry - she likes Balmoral...

Lucifer - she'll probably drown in it...she can go from there to the Vatican you know..

Sherry - seriously...

Lucifer - yes underground reptile tunnels...we party at the Vatican together...

Sherry - omg...

Lucifer - LOL...

Lucifer - and she has her own set up there...her little basement of horrors...it's almost as good as mine...she has a maze of tunnels down there and she lets humans loose in it...they try to find their way out and escape the lizards...it's funny, we tape it and watch it...watch them get cornered and eaten..

Lucifer - you're quiet..

Sherry - sitting here shaking my head..

Lucifer - laughs...

Lucifer - they all like to participate...family affair....

Lucifer - if you're like us, you think it's awesome...

Sherry - I'm not like you...

Lucifer - you destroyed the city under Buckingham, we had to make new playgrounds...

Sherry - what's at Kensington,

Lucifer - nothing, but you can get to Balmoral from Kensington,

Sherry - somehow that doesn't surprise me...

Lucifer - laughs, nothing should by now..

Sherry - what's that new base the CIA built in VA...then acted like they were moving their headquarters...

Lucifer - that was to throw people off...that new base got half destroyed but they rebuilt it by now I'm sure...

Sherry - what about that NSA facility in Utah...the one they were threatening to shut the water off to...

Lucifer - yeah the government didn't want them stealing their people in Utah....playing hard ball...or thought they would...

Sherry - that's connected to NV by now..

Lucifer - yep...they needed a secondary route away from there in case they needed it...that desert could get flooded again...people think it's just a spy facility but there's a 10 level base under it for backup

Sherry - why is everything always 10 levels?

Lucifer - 10 known, 3 hidden, the way it always is...I don't know they just stuck with that...easier to keep with the same floor mats when you're building stuff...make it look military, people don't ask questions..

Sherry - what is it really...lizard fests?

Lucifer - usually...especially the last 3 hidden levels..

Lucifer - we're starting to put mazes in them since that's proven to be so much fun...escape the lizard...LOL...

Sherry - what else do you do...

Sherry - when you put snakes in people you can overtake them can't you.. that's how you overtake them and operate through them..

Lucifer - yes. I can't believe you figured that one out...the snake...I can act through the snake, since that's what I am...

Sherry - what about the lizard thing they implant behind peoples eye..

Lucifer - that's how they operate,

Sherry - the reptiles..

Lucifer - yes...and I go through via the snake...it's the Brotherhood of the Serpent, or Serpent Brotherhood, not lizard, they worship me direct... they can worship me direct or get taken over by the reptiles, I don't care...

Sherry - you were changed from them because of the curses at the Garden....

Lucifer - yes.. a little bit...but they're still mine

Lucifer - I can't believe you figure that stuff out, you're pretty smart..

Sherry - I'm nothing on my own, it's dad...he reveals things to me...

Lucifer - you're getting to dangerous...laughs...

Lucifer - it's all good, no one cares anymore...we don't even have to hide because we're in charge now...no one can run from us...

Sherry - tick tick tick....

Lucifer - yep it's almost time, it's almost time for the next phase...I can't wait! Candle burning time!

Chapter Thirteen

Interview With The Devil - Part 10

05-04-16

Lucifer - it takes her forever..

    Sherry - ok I'm ready..

    Lucifer - ha!

    Sherry - had to get some coffee..

    Lucifer - how can you drink that garbage..

    Sherry - everything's garbage..

    Sherry- ok I want to ask you a few questions on some people...

    Lucifer - people? They're all mine..

    Sherry - yeah well I know these are...ok tell me about this gang you keep shoving down our throats...Kardashians, Beyonce, Kenye West, JZ...

    Lucifer - laughs...oh brother...seriously...they are all mine...and they're all huge money makers, that's why we sell them, because people are buying them...

    Lucifer - ok first one, Kardashians...the mother is ours, she signed the dotted line, but the other 3 aren't, we had to replace them with look-alikes and we've already used dozens of them by now...

    Sherry - ok I already knew that maybe Lillith told me...

    Lucifer - probably, she's the one that loves playing with Hollywood people...

Lucifer - Beyonce...she's a lab rat...we've controlled her forever, her dad was her handler...he gave her to us at an early age...she does what we program her to do, sometimes it malfunctions like at that basketball game...that was funny and people didn't say anything...we control the media...there was some videos on it but people are stupid...we can always count on that... a few made it obvious but most don't listen to the few..

Lucifer - Kenya West - he's a little punk...I hate that bitch...he thinks he's got a bigger pair than mine and that's just wrong...wrong...he's close to blasphemy with me...that's why he's having money problems...laughs... wait till I take it all away...he needs to shut up and start serving rather than running his mouth all the time.

Lucifer - JZ - that guy's a lab rat, we use him to recruit others and control the whack job we married him to...laughs...he stepped up so we use him...made him filthy rich to to keep the others in line...I hate that rap garbage, as you say, 'rap crap' ...but it's useful, fills up the prisons, keeps the slaves well...slaves...we fill their heads with self pity, hate, anger, violence, they eat it up...they're idiots...but what do I care...

Sherry - what about Jennifer Hudson? She sacrificed her mother, sister, nephew, for Weight Watchers commercials and an Oscar?

Lucifer - laughs..

Sherry - I mean seriously? Wasn't she supposed to get elevated to Whitney Houston status? What happened with that?

Lucifer - she's got attitude...that's what happened...and when you start mouthing against us we'll shut you up and sit you down...and that's what happened with that...too much attitude...I hate attitude...that's why I hate that Kenya punk...

Sherry - I heard this story about Tom Cruise and his daughter Surrie... he fell asleep in his room, lost his human form and turned into his reptile self, and the daughter walked into his room and saw him sleeping...and ran out screaming her daddy was a monster...is that true?

Lucifer - laughs...probably...he's one of us...but he hangs around with that Scientology group of lizards, they like to keep separate from the Hollywood group...we gave him $ hundreds of millions no one is worth that much...so we took him over...we'll use clones if we have to...just to keep his name going...and keep the money coming in, they use him to fund that Scientology stuff...that's one of our branches...you ruined the headquarters in FL...

Sherry - laughs...LOL...how'd you know

Lucifer - I heard about it, they piss your name...they hate you..

Sherry - LOL laughs...

Lucifer - you leave your mark everywhere, people are getting pissed off....

Sherry - laughs...good...

Sherry - what about Jim Carrey, don't tell me that's the real one in Hollywood. I know what happened in 2012...laughs....

Lucifer - yeah that's not him...but you knew that...the problem with his clones is they feed off the original one's brain...and if the original started to turn against his controllers or us, the clones end up with attitudes to... it's something you always have to deal with...you prop them up for some spotlight then keep them hidden away..

Sherry - isn't he the High Priest in LA

Lucifer - they've had to work around him

Sherry - did Robert Shapiro take over?

Lucifer - He doesn't want it, he likes being the second man in charge...

Sherry - didn't he kill Michael Jackson on the altar?

Lucifer - (angry)...how did you know that!!

Sherry - laughs...because I know...

Lucifer - wow, that was secret, buried...for a long time...you're going to turn heads with that one!

Sherry - they sacrificed Michael Jackson...had him dress up as that demon thing he portrayed in his video Thriller...then they killed him didn't they....

Lucifer - wow...wow...you're good...oh man...if that gets out...wow... you're getting way to dangerous with the info...they're gonna flip their chairs...course I would usually some something much more vulgar but you get the meaning..

Sherry - laughs...amazing..

Sherry - ok so let's talk OJ Simpson...

Lucifer - oh there's another one...haha you're lighting torches now...

Sherry - whatever that means...

Sherry - tell me about him...

Lucifer - what do you know...

Sherry - I think he was involved but I think he was covering for his son...

Lucifer - laughs..

Lucifer - he actually had that planned for a while...made sure the limo guy showed up to take him to the airport so he'd have an alibi...

Sherry - was his son involved

Lucifer - yes...he was the second man there...but he parked way down across the street and then took off...she was their sacrifice...just to stay alive because OJ would never join the Illuminati but they were blackmailing him to give them a sacrifice because of the success he'd had...they killed that Kardashian because he couldn't get OJ to join and he wouldn't sacrifice his wife or kids. They told OJ if he didn't give them a sacrifice, because he already knew to much, they were going to take one of his kids. So the 2 (OJ and his son) planned it and then killed her...they saw that guy, Goldman but went ahead and killed him to because it would throw it off that she was the sole target, they were going to try and make it look like a murder suicide but it got all messed up because they didn't have time to plan it through, he was a spur of the moment addition to it, the whole thing was brutal. I loved all the blood there...nice sacrifice... huge mess...notice how that Al guy disappeared? He was involved to.

Sherry - was he really..

Lucifer - yes...he knew about it...helped them plan it..

Sherry - tell me about Donald Trump...I liked the old Donald. They already killed him didn't they...

Lucifer - you were right about his youngest son, but they're all 3 mine...so doesn't matter...(youngest son is a Jesuit)

Lucifer - why is the oldest kept out of the spotlight...

Lucifer - he wants it that way...so the younger one steps up, he's one of us anyway...you saw it in his eyes..

Sherry - yes...

Lucifer - Donald was mind wired..

Sherry - omg I was thinking that the other day...

Lucifer - yep...there's clones too already...but the original was mind wired, they're trying something new...see if it works....

Sherry - so he's the new breed of tech slaves?

Lucifer - laughs...yep...course he's never left alone...no one thought he'd have a chance of getting in as president but we got our bases covered, he's one of us anyway

Sherry - so then why did you mind wire him..

Lucifer - he's a loose cannon, another one who thinks he can run his own life apart from us, not going to happen...we're always the bosses... you saw his black eye..

Sherry - yep...Joan Rivers funeral

Lucifer - yep...I can't believe you stole that one from us!!!!!! That made me so mad!

Sherry - laughs...LOL..yep..

Lucifer - how did that happen?

Sherry - she was in a coma...I don't know if it was for as long as they said it was...but when she was in it dad let me reach out to her...because she wasn't dead yet...once they're dead they're gone...but she wasn't dead so I got to talk to her for a while...

Lucifer - that was incredible....I was stunned, stunned...

Lucifer - she was part of that NY group to...you literally stole that one from me...I was shocked..

Sherry - she's happy...

Lucifer - and her daughter hates you, they all do...

Sherry - why does she hate me...look what I did for her mother...

Lucifer - maybe she doesn't know, I don't know...you got your crap all over the place out there and they hate you for that...

Sherry - LOL laughs...the Orgone...LOL...

Lucifer - you have no idea...you would be amazed how many people would kill you in a heart beat if they had the chance...

Sherry - laughs...that tells me how many possessed people and lizards are out there because Orgone doesn't affect humans...laughs...

Lucifer - well you know there's not many humans left anywhere in the spotlight so what do you think...

Lucifer - that's why were going with the mind wires...we control their brains, we wire them up instead of them having to use boxes like Bush Jr. did...it's like a wireless system they're going with...

Sherry - so it's like robots...wireless controlled robots...

Lucifer - yep...how did you know about that?

Sherry - I was seeing it in the codes...wondered what it was...

Sherry - he looks wired, looks fake, his emotions are fake...he looks like he's waiting for transmissions...it's weird just watching him...

Lucifer - lizards don't want to get trapped in human bodies now since your proclamation against them...and he's 70 years old...

Sherry - LOL...so that worked eh?

Lucifer - you got them all scared...you do so much crap to my people...

Sherry - laughs..

Lucifer - no one wants to have to possess anyone now, so we're going with the wireless tech...and the temporal bodies are restrictive to them... they don't like them...they don't last long enough, you eat them up with your flesh eating plagues...it's getting ridiculous the amount of damage your doing....

Sherry- LOL...good...good...I do all this stuff and then it takes me forever to get confirmations, hear the results...I hear them from dad but it's awesome hearing it from the horses themselves..

Lucifer - oh you wait little girl...or woman I should say...your day's coming...it's coming..

Sherry - laughs..

Sherry - so I hear there was a fire fight in my backyard Sat night...UFO shot a (USAF) jet plane down not to far from here...

Lucifer - well I don't know but I wouldn't doubt it...there's always fights in that area...always...that's why they cover it with heavy clouds and black out tech so much...to hide the fighting...and just to piss you off because you love to look at the sky...I hear about that...

Sherry - laughs...I wish Yahushua would come get me already!

Lucifer - so do I!

Sherry - laughs...

Sherry - so is Madonna a wife of yours

Lucifer - she's been mine for a long time...

Lucifer - you know why she looks so old...because she drinks so much blood...

Sherry - I didn't know that made you old...

Lucifer - yeah it will...some people have an adverse affect to it...ages them...so does astral travel and she likes to spy on people...

Sherry - I don't even know anyone she hangs out with...what group does she hang with

Lucifer - she's involved with the NY and LA groups...she's a spy, enforcer, that's why you see her recruit people in publicly to the Illuminati... she's a witch...

Sherry - what's her sacrifice...

Lucifer - she does public rituals...public initiations...her concerts, TV appearances...all designed to publicly initiate the masses into the Illuminati...she pushes that whole thing...it brings her a lot of reward...but if she ever loses her appeal they'll get rid of her to make room for someone else...they're trying to prime Beyonce to take over that role but people don't seem to be taking to her...

Sherry - the persona they push of her is bigger than she is...I don't see what the big deal is with her...she's a puppet...and they always prop her...it gets ridiculous...the media never shuts up about her...

Lucifer - because they're trying to raise her up...public acceptance...

Sherry - it's nauseating...like what we're they saying yesterday, we all live in Beyonce's world...blah blah...it's nauseating...she's the queen of a toilet, nothing else...

Lucifer - LOL laughs...

Sherry - and the Kardashians...I'm so sick of them...it's constant constant TV garbage on them...

Lucifer - they don't have anyone else...they use them as an example to everyone else, the fame and fortune you can get to sign the dotted line, they're bait...

Sherry- it's backfiring, everyone's sick of them...

Lucifer - laughs....someone's always buying..

Chapter Fourteen

Interview With The
Devil - Part 11

05-05-16

Lucifer - it's my turn!
    Sherry - ok, ok hang on...
    Lucifer - what are you doing, running?!
    Sherry - ok I'm ready...running to where? Maybe the fridge...
    Lucifer - laughs...haha
    Lucifer - ok it's my turn,
    Sherry - alright alright alright...
    Lucifer - what is that thing you always wear...
    Sherry - what thing? My pendent? It's an Orgone pendent...
    Lucifer - what does it do?
    Sherry - it repels evil mother---------bonkers like you
    Lucifer -ha! dad stopped you I heard that!
    Sherry - LOL...yep...have to watch myself talking to you!
    Lucifer - what do you mean it repels them?
    Sherry - it's our Orgone so they hate it...it aggravates and irritates
them...lizard people who come to close to us when we're wearing these
hate it...they look at you really mad...it's funny..
    Lucifer - because it's annoying
    Sherry - yes, to them, if your a human you wouldn't even notice it...

Lucifer - so it only bothers us...

Sherry - basically

Lucifer - ah, ingenious...

Sherry - I think so..

Lucifer - what does it do to demons?

Sherry - keeps them away, they won't come near it...they run...

Lucifer - hmmmm...

Lucifer - you disrupt things with that..

Sherry - laughs...you mean like Benny Hinn crusades? LOL...

Lucifer - yes! And others...

Sherry - laughs...they're such fakes...it's really obvious when we keep the demons away and they won't show up to help them perform their charades..

Lucifer - hmmm

Sherry - is Madonna a vampire?

Lucifer - what? hmm...she does it all...if she can't get it (blood) she'll just take it...she don't care...she's one of us...she likes to go on prowls...I've seen her...

Sherry - does she go with Lilith?

Lucifer - laughs...that would be harder, but I'm sure they've pal'd around with each other on a hunt fest...she's no stranger to the hunt and kill...

Sherry - what about Selena Gomez, I heard she was a vampire..

Lucifer - yeah she is...

Sherry - what about Justin Bieber, I heard he has red demon eyes that glare ...

Lucifer - ha! He has an ancient one inside him...they called up one of the ancients at a ritual and put it inside him, or her, whatever, you had that one right, he was born a girl...

Sherry - I'm always right...

Lucifer - laughs...more than you know, it's funny..

Sherry - ha! Coming from you that's amusing...but whatever,

Sherry - what about Charlie Sheen?

Lucifer - he's one of us, but he causes a lot of problems because he's getting psycho...

Sherry - you mean uncontrollable?

Lucifer - laughs...he better watch it...

Lucifer - his father is a Jesuit priest...(Martin Sheen)...but you already knew that..

Sherry - yeah so I've heard..

Lucifer - I heard you like the MMA scene

Sherry - I love MMA...(mixed martial arts)

Lucifer - because you were a fighter ...Shaz is one of the best...no one can beat her...she's got a huge sword, thing must weigh 200 lbs...most can't even pick up her sword!

Sherry - laughs...dad gave me that

Lucifer - I know! That thing is huge, and about solid gold...suits you..

Sherry - ha...I miss home..

Lucifer - well I wish you'd get your angel ass off earth and back there, and get out of my hair...

Sherry - laughs..

Lucifer - dad told me things might be heating up soon...

Sherry - oh yeah..? I've been trying to figure things out but I've been to caught up with this stuff to get into the (Bible) codes to much...and they're (Ashtar group) always wishy washy so I can't be missing to much!

Lucifer - ha! yeah well...someone's going to make a move soon, I can feel it...them or dad...

Sherry - I hope it's dad...I could care less about your own idiots...unless it's them being the cause of holding things up for us...

Lucifer - dad said watch for this weekend...might be some fireworks somewhere..

Sherry - fireworks? Are they going to try and blow up my house again?

Lucifer - laughs! yeah code speak! LOL...laughs...I don't know, probably not, I don't think anyone can get near there!

Sherry - good...I don't need the aggravation...I got enough to deal with..

Lucifer - so did you tell Marilyn she's going to be the mediator?

Sherry - yes...but I told her probably between me and earth people because only dad can control you and I...

Lucifer = LOL ..laughs...! yeah I can believe that! LOL...well you never know....

Sherry - yeah we'll see how it pans out..

Lucifer - Lilith wanted me to ask you how her bitches are doing

Sherry - still going to hell that I can see..

Lucifer - laughs! LOL...oh that's low...

Sherry - reality....

Lucifer - laughs...I'll tell her...laughs...that's bad that's bad...

Lucifer - Lillith says you're a bitch..

Sherry - oh well, I'll wear it like a charm bracelet..

Lucifer - ok next thing...

Sherry - what...

Lucifer - dad said you've been posting this stuff online

Sherry - yeah He wants me to get it out there...let people see what they're dealing with, what the past was, present is, and future's going to be...

Lucifer - quite an eye opener for them I'm sure...but I don't care...I took over then, I rule now, and I'm going to be worshiped as god in the future...that's all they need to know!

Sherry - you're a legend up your own ass..

Lucifer - LOL...laughs...LOLOLOL

Sherry - (sorry dad...)

Lucifer - LOL laughs...you are such a bitch...but that was funny...credit where it's due..

Sherry - laughs...just truth and reality...and perspective! That's what this is about...perspective!

Lucifer - so what's it doing there now?

Sherry - it's raining like usual...it's always raining, or cloudy, just gloom and more gloom...

Lucifer - ha, yeah, they control the weather, have full control of it...they can do what they want, anywhere..

Sherry - yawn,....tired of all your games and charades...if it's not one thing it's another...

Lucifer - we control all aspects of earth..

Sherry - but your own judgment that's coming...that's going to be epic!

Lucifer - so is yours!

Lucifer - Lilith says watch out bitch she's coming for you!

Sherry - she already has...62,000 offenses...what's a few more...

Lucifer - laughs...just the tip I'm sure...

Sherry - her people keep trying to troll my Facebook...they have nothing of interest to even say...they're all so boring and dumb, they recycle the same garbage and diatribes...

Lucifer - I'm surprised you even have it

Sherry - there's more of your people on it (my Facebook) than dad's..

Lucifer - LOL I can believe that...

Sherry - they hacked my account this morning and tried keeping me off it all day, so I asked dad to track down the hackers, who was doing what, if it was hackers or Zuckerburg at FB messing with me...it was hackers at the Pentagon....so we blew up the computer of the guy that was messing with me...

Lucifer - laughs...oh man...you've blown up so much of their stuff... satellites...computers...star ships, planes...heard you even got a train!

Sherry - LOL laughs...oh yeah...I didn't hear of that one...

Lucifer - you were the cause of some kind of wreck in W. VA. when they were clearing that base out in Moundsville you destroyed!

Sherry - LOL..yeah...that was a huge one...I heard about a train fire or derailment or something but didn't know it was the Orgone...

Lucifer - yeah it did something...when I heard about it my people said to mark that one for Shriner...I laughed...you never stop!

Sherry - I never will...

Lucifer - so let's see...how come you don't do any radio shows...interviews with my people..?

Sherry - because I'm blacklisted and they're afraid of me..

Lucifer - laughs...oh yeah...I sent that order out didn't I...

Sherry - patting yourself on the back?

Lucifer - amazed at my own genius at times...dad doesn't realize how I control everything down there...

Sherry - I'm sure it hasn't passed by His attention...He knows what you do...

Lucifer - laughs...He's actually been pretty civil to me lately...

Sherry - you make Him very angry...you make everyone very angry..

Lucifer - laughs...so what's your next plans..

Sherry - I have none, I want to leave! If I even sneeze that could be the cause of another one of your retarded delays...I'm waiting for them to arrive, but I'm getting tired of waiting...I can't just sit here and twiddle my thumbs waiting..

Lucifer - well that's exactly what you should do...they're watching you...

Sherry - I know...so get it on already...tired of this, I'm going to start blowing up satellites again...

Lucifer - laughs...my people don't need them, but the gov's do..

Sherry - I know...I'm being very patient...very patient....

Lucifer - didn't you destroy Musk's satellites? The ones Bush owned?

Sherry - yep...they were pissing me off...

Lucifer - LOL...they'll learn Shaz has a temper...

Sherry - I'm not even Shaz here...but dad has my back..

Lucifer - same person...2 peas in a pod...when you come back the war will be on and it will be epic..

Sherry - have you done any time jumping...traveling..

Lucifer - everything always changes, you can't rely on that...

Sherry - right, it's like the codes..

Lucifer - they tried to do time traveling on you but there were blocks...they couldn't even find you...they hit walls on everyone they were looking for...

Sherry - because the future isn't set in stone, people can change things...albeit events stay the same, or will stay the same for this time-line... Bible prophecy will play out...

Lucifer - are you going to go back to NY?

Sherry - I need a new horse for that..

Lucifer - laughs..

Lucifer - dad said I'll meet you in NY someday

Sherry - yeah He told me the same thing...but that's as Shaz...not the here and now...

Lucifer - ah yeah...that's how I see it to...

Lucifer - are all the angels returning...(the Elect, angels in the flesh)

Sherry - I don't know...I don't know how it's going to play out with the others...I'm sure they will...we're all going to have different things to do ...have our own assignments, whatever, they've been talking about the Madrid fault line lately...I think they're trying to prepare people for that thing getting ready to blow in case it does...

Lucifer - the Madrid...hmm..that runs north and south of America right...

Sherry - yes...Great Lakes to gulf of Mexico..

Lucifer - you're little 6th Seal...break the country in half...?

Sherry - I'm hoping that's it...I assumed it was...feels like it, feels right..

Sherry - you've got all your people thinking they're going to be taken off the earth before the chaos hits...

Lucifer - laughs...yeah that's what we tell them...

Sherry - are you...

Lucifer - not possible...if we take them off as humans they come back as reptile hosts...just ask the astronauts...laughs...

Sherry - I warned the New Agers about ending up as meat in alien freezers..

Lucifer - laughs...yep they do...and will be...

Sherry - what about all this gov crap where you have practice runs of loading them up in UFOs...heard about that years ago...let me think that's when Condoleezza Rice was working in the White House...something about all them leaving because they thought something was going to happen...

Lucifer - LOL yeah they do that when they want to round them all up and infect them with our parasite hosts or a lizard just wants to take them over..

Sherry - what's this about Congress several years ago all getting rounded up and getting on a plane to go to a funeral in Florida and then went missing for two days...

Lucifer - laughs...yep, we round them up for whatever reason and just take over them...that's much easier to do them all at once...

Sherry - I thought I saw a bunch of them at a base in Alaska several years ago. I saw them separated, men, women, kids...the kids were shipped off to China to be sex slaves, they forced the men to admit to their wives what scumbag child rapists and murderers they actually were...then they cloned the women and men and killed the originals off... what the heck was that about?

Lucifer - laughs...we do that a lot...especially with gov people...we can't have loose cannons running around...especially every time the elections change Congress...but now we have it so that even candidates are all ours...you can't even run unless your pre-approved...no more surprises and idiots to have to deal with who think they're going to go in and make changes to the way we do things...they just cause problems...now we have control of all that...man you're talking about stuff that happened before Obama took office...because since then we've taken control of every aspect of elections, DC. you name it, down to local elections...course we already controlled the Presidency...we always do...

Sherry - do you have this much fun in Europe?

Lucifer - laughs...it's already ours...been ours since the Dark Ages... it's always stayed dark in Europe...never changed...that's why all you little Jew Israel assess took off to America...to get away from our control...but we just took over that too...we were right behind you ...

Sherry - tell me about Montauk (northern Long Island, NY)

Lucifer - Montauk...oh that place is crazy, another fun house...

Sherry - doesn't DARPA run it

Lucifer - yeah...but it's all reptiles...it's a fun house for them...and they do all kinds of crazy stuff there. There's a gate there. They cross breed there...they time travel...they do all kinds of time travel experiments there. A lot of people leave and never come back I hear...they get lost in the time warps, those time travel gates are crazy...and there's a lot of stuff that comes through them...so we tag them and send them back out to see where they go. That's how we target creatures we want to bring in for later...once they're tagged we can pull them back in. I want to know where the nests are...where the civilizations of them are..

Sherry - like you did on Nibiru...

Lucifer - yeah we did the same thing there...but we had maps on Nibiru...I had to start over here...

Sherry - so before the onslaught hits everyone thinks they'll be protected, that you're going to take them off the earth ...

Lucifer - laughs...I say it they believe it...they should know better...*uck them all ...I'm not saving anyone from what's coming. It brings them in, gives them some kind of assurance and protection because they're all the ones helping me pull this stuff off...but they're on their own when SHTF...

Sherry - what about the UN and White House...

Lucifer - laughs...same thing...humans are on their own, I can't help them...wouldn't anyway...they're all gonna be thinking "I should have listened to Sherry Shriner" and I'm going to be laughing saying *uck you...*uck you all...and I'll be laughing as I head out the door...so to speak...

Sherry - do you have any secret places where you all meet? I heard you meet in the 5th dimension...is that true..

Lucifer - hmm...the reptiles do...they can leave when the human body is sleeping and go for a while...because they don't sleep...humans who astral travel can...and of course we have our soul sucking tech that can pull a person's soul out of their body and we can take it where we want...

Sherry - yeah I've heard of what they call the cloning centers doing that to people...making them show up there at night for all their stuff...that Marshall guy talks about it..

Lucifer - yeah he's one of us...we let him reveal a bunch of stuff... anyone who speaks out like that and they're still alive, they're one of us... except you...dad protects His own...but we let stuff get revealed just to get the ball rolling on disclosure...people always wonder when disclosure is going to take place and it's around them every day....they don't realize it...they think someone's going to stand up with a bullhorn and give a speech...not gonna happen...we use regular everyday people to expose and disclose things...

Sherry - yeah I was already onto that...

Lucifer - yeah you would be...but everyone else is stupid...we just sit and laugh at the in-your-face stuff already exposed or revealed and people don't even believe it...they'll fight you to the death over what they think truth is, they have no idea what it is...and when we try to give it to them they reject it...

Sherry - I know. I know...

Lucifer - laughs..

Sherry - only dad can sort this mess out...it's always been like this... but back in the day there wasn't 8 billion people on the earth. It's a different day and age. It's the end of the age....of ages..

Chapter Fifteen

Interview With The Devil - Part 12

05-07-16

Transgender Revolution

Sherry - you're so impatient..

Lucifer - I've been waiting forever!

Sherry - they had something out about Donald Trump's mother being a tranny because of her big head and little body..

Lucifer - laughs, yep! They got rid of the original, replaced her with that thing

Sherry - how do they come up with all these kids to make tranny's look like they're just normal parents..

Lucifer - they make them (the kids) in labs, they mix them up, 3 party DNA then someone carries them...surrogate...a lot of surrogates are used...man we've been doing this for 50 years, you people are soo slow ...

Sherry- ok I'm going to ask you if these people are transgenders:

Sherry - Tammy Wynette..

Lucifer - yep

Sherry - Faith Hill

Lucifer - yep

Sherry - Tim McGraw

Lucifer - oh that' a good one, yep, the men are harder to figure out than the women..

Sherry - are you serious...omg...Tim McGraw?

Lucifer - yep that was a Tina!

Sherry - laughs..

Sherry - Amal Clooney

Lucifer - LOL laughs...yep

Sherry - Melania Trump

Lucifer - yep...from Lebanon, one of our few masterpieces from that dump

Sherry - Mariah Carey

Lucifer - hmmm...no she's normal but she's a witch, and she's a MK Ultra lab rat

Sherry - Bruce Springstein...

Lucifer - laughs...oh man he's a mix, reptoid, female, MK Ultra..

Sherry - Prince

Lucifer - prince was gay, he was a male but he was MK Ultra too...like most of them are,

Sherry - Barbara Bush

Lucifer - Crowley's kid...yeah that was a Ben, made an uglier Barbie... that guy was a freak, he was worse than me,

Sherry - that's hard to imagine. How's he like hell?

Lucifer - oh he's in one of the worst parts...he was in the carnival for a long time, you know the ferris wheel stuff..

Sherry - yeah..

Lucifer - hard telling where he is now

Sherry - is that the worst place? Where's the tables at?

Lucifer - that's called the Lab...he was there to for a long time..

Sherry - serves him right,

Sherry - is there a hook room?

Lucifer - laughs, yep! I got one of those at the Vatican, I got all that stuff at the Vatican, well I got the maze, lab, and hook room...

Sherry - gross.

Sherry- Beyonce

Lucifer - LOL, yep

Sherry - JZ

Lucifer - LOL yep..

Sherry - are you serious...JZ??

Lucifer - yep! born a girl, we start changing them immediately and groom them...they all become lab rats after that...we control them....

Lucifer - we turned that whole macho hood crowd into fags with our transgender revolution...we influence all the blacks through them and they follow them into anything we lead them into!

Sherry - George Clooney?

Lucifer - no but he likes his little tranny (Amal), he's gay, so is Brad Pitt..

Sherry - what about Angelina Jolie...

Lucifer - she's MK Ultra...her dad is a freak...he's one of us, long time...he plays in soap drama...he gave her to us as his sacrifice..

Sherry - Kylie Jenner and the other one...(Kendall)

Lucifer- the 2 younger ones are boys...they were Kris' sacrifice and Bruce's....

Sherry - then why did he (Bruce Jenner) change later? I thought he was promoting the whole revolution as a sacrifice...

Lucifer - he is, but it's his service to us...everyone has to have a service...it's not just about success and what they do, they have to serve us to...

Sherry - you keep them busy...

Lucifer - heck yeah...

Sherry - what's Justin Bieber's service?

Lucifer - he's a hired male lesbo...whatever you want to call it! LOL...women pay for him...so do men...and he's a setup, when it comes out he's a transgender all the little girls will flock to get it done...or boys, whatever, he influences a lot of kids. that's what we use the pop stars for...influence...

Sherry - what about Miley Cyrus

Lucifer - oh man you busted us on that one...she's been gone a long time...I don't know how you figured that one out...(the original was killed years ago)

Sherry - I went to her in the 5th (dimension)..

Lucifer - I wouldn't doubt it...yeah she's gone..

Sherry - that one that took over, is Lauren her name?

Lucifer - I think so...not sure...she's more a freak than Miley ever was.... and she has fun with it..

Sherry - I was going to ask you Judge Judy has a really really weird aura..

Lucifer - man she's looney...she's a witch..

Sherry - is she a vampire because I get that her spirit is, but her human part isn't...it's odd....

Lucifer - ha! she's controlled by an old soul...the witches put that into her...it's prob her that's the vampire...but she can go in other realms when Judy's sleeping or whatever...funny you picked that up...

Sherry - Judge Joe Brown...

Lucifer - he's one of us....

Sherry - he's got a serpent...he just feels evil..

Lucifer - laughs...yeah he's got one...he hates you...

Sherry - laughs...LOL...he was with my clone...I saw that...sitting at a table ..that was odd

Lucifer - you saw that??!!

Sherry - yeah...with two others...just talking...he wouldn't even look at her, had his back to her...

Lucifer - laughs...yeah you got to much light, even your clones are pathetic...it's nauseating, annoying..

Sherry - laughs...good!

Sherry - what was the whole deal with the playboy mansion and Hugh Heffner

Lucifer - he was a pimp...the girls were presidential sex toys but we had no need for them anymore because they were all gay or liked kids! So they kept up the charade for a while and used them as couriers, prostitutes to foreign leaders etc...but even they're gay and like kids...everyone's a pedophile now we turned them on to that...or gay..

Sherry - they closed down the mansion I heard..

Lucifer - laughs...yeah the charade's over...now they just need orphanages and child sex trades...laughs..

Sherry- Brooke Shields

Lucifer - she was right up there as one of the first ones! She was Bob Hope's little boy toy! ha!

Lucifer - a lot of celebrities we killed then replaced with tranny's...so even if they were born normal we switched them over later..

Sherry - what about Hollywood A list...they're all cross dressing...men are wearing dresses, females suits...

Lucifer - it's part of the initiation into our transgender revolution...go gay or transgender...course most of them just went gay...but if they ever get to that level and give us problems, we'd just kill them and replace them with a tranny at this point to push our gender revolution..

Sherry - why are you pushing a gender revolution..

Lucifer - because gay isn't bad enough anymore...we push the limits..

Sherry - it's nauseating..

Lucifer - laughs...LOL...it puts more energy into the mix...celebrities are having kids offering them to us for gender swaps rather than having to sacrifice...it's working out well..

Sherry - do they all have a say in it

Lucifer - no, not if they're lab rats and already ours, we can take their kids and do what we want and they have nothing to say about it... seriously most of them don't even care anymore, especially the ones we already switched out...a surrogate has the kid then gives them it to raise..

Sherry - what about Brittney Spears boys

Lucifer - they're already ours....

Sherry - what are you doing to them

Lucifer - I don't know what they're going to do to those two, probably be gay...or wearing women's clothes like Jadin Smith....ha! now that's a messed up family! laughs...we own them all, they're all puppets to us...

Sherry- is this part of signing the dotted line..

Lucifer - it is for Hollywood. We have the most fun with them..

Sherry - dad was showing me something about all the fakes out there... they have those huge indents in their chests right below their necks...their voice boxes...

Lucifer - laughs yep! Those are tranny's....clones, androids, whatever,

Sherry - I noticed normal people don't have necks like that, they look like they have tubes inside them and then a huge indent at the base..

Lucifer - laughs...yep...good catch....I'm impressed...you can tell them apart when you know what to look for...that's one of the things, also the eyes and for tranny's the biggest things to notice are the size of their heads to their shoulders, hands, feet, it's hard to hide a man's big feet as a woman, or small feet as a man!

Lucifer - we're pushing them through the TV shows...they don't get media attention until they're 'proven'....they've proven themselves to be worthy of our attention and time...we're already filling up commercials and audiences with them...

Sherry - I noticed that, I always look at them now...

Lucifer - laughs..

Sherry - what's the big forehead syndrome?

Sherry - so many people are getting huge foreheads?

Lucifer - that's an adverse affect of the drugs they're taking...chemicals...could be steroids or transgender meds..

Chapter Sixteen

Interview With The Devil - Part 13

05-08-16

Lucifer - the last phase begins when you leave...

Lucifer - dad said if earth wasn't big enough for the 3 of us...then heaven wouldn't be either...

Sherry - LOLOLOLOLOL

Lucifer - LOLOLOOL

Lucifer - He's got that right...

Lucifer - when you leave to come up here we'll (Lucifer & Lillith) leave to go back down there...

Lucifer - you'll be up there for a while so we can set up, then the fun begins....

Sherry - the fun being I return..

Lucifer - yep...

Lucifer - and I begin my candle burning fest! I can't wait!

Sherry - I was going to ask you because last time the angels who had your tattoo on their hands, your stamp, were protected from the creatures...your people won't be protected this time will they..

Lucifer - no...they're on their own....

Sherry - all of them

Lucifer - yep, every one of them....

Lucifer - I'm not protecting anyone but me and mine

Sherry - who is 'me and mine'

Lucifer - me!

Sherry - Laughs...LOL...I figured..

Sherry - what about all these people who spend their entire lives worshiping you and serving you...

Lucifer - it's game over at that point...they're on their own, I'm on my own, everyone's on their own..

Sherry - what about your little pawn beasts that will be running around...antichrist and false prophet.

Lucifer - characters on the stage...after the candle burning phase I really don't care what they do...you know what this earth is going to be like then...

Sherry - yep..

Lucifer - I know Yash (Yahushua)+ is going to return, try to reclaim that dump in the Middle East. I'll be ready for Him...I don't want it but He isn't going to get it either...it's going to be target practice for us!

Sherry - you're all pathetic...you'll all be destroyed...there will be no fight...LOL laughs...you can't defend yourself against the Kingdom of Heaven, you have no defense, just destruction waiting for yourselves..

Lucifer - whatever, we don't care what you think..

Sherry - laughs...

Lucifer - are you going to be with Him

Sherry - I'll be right behind Him...

Sherry - He'll conquer earth once and for all, He'll come from the background and put an end to your sorry existence for another 1000 years...and all yours will be round up and fuel for the fire...I actually feel sorry for them but I've done what I can...they're so stupid there's no hope for them..

Lucifer - laughs...you get what you can while you can...then it's over, another game begins,

Sherry - after the 1,000 years...

Lucifer - yes. I'll be back to destroy your little set up on earth for the 3rd time...even I know what your little book says since we hacked most of it...some things dad said we couldn't change, most stuff people could figure out on their own but that's when we stood up and took over and did their thinking for them, they believe what we tell them...

Sherry - I don't...

Lucifer - you left the box, plenty more still in it.

Sherry - I've got stuff from Lillith's perspective to reveal, most don't even believe she exists....

Lucifer - we've had more success with the churches than we could have ever dreamt possible..

Lucifer - we're going to control the money, the food, the property (land)...no one can have food, property or land who aren't loyal to us... that's where the fighting will be in America, cuz everyone has ownership or thinks they do of their own land, houses etc...but we're going to take it from them....if they aren't loyal to us they can't keep it...we'll go door to door...if they don't have my mark they'll be rounded up like cattle...

Sherry - taken to the FEMA camps..

Lucifer - yes..

Lucifer - a lot we'll just tag and bag so to speak...we'll kill them..

Lucifer - but they'll have some fun with the select few they decide to (have some fun with), we'll get them to take the mark...the ones who have a lot of light, we'll torture them...the ones who are mine anyway we'll just bag them...no one cares about them...

Sherry - is this when you're pulling out the guillotines..

Lucifer - yeah they'll be at the camps at first, later they'll be on every corner...laughs....we'll set them up at court houses, or even in parks, wherever needed... immediate judgment for those who refuse to join my kingdom!

Sherry - are they doing this everywhere

Lucifer - yes worldwide scale...

Lucifer - we'll have armies go out, in America it'll be quite easy because everything's already controlled from state to local levels...we just move into the local levels and take over the communities door to door... one at a time...you get the picture...

Sherry - yeah...I hope people are locked and loaded.

Lucifer - laughs...yeah that'll be a problem in America...that's why we'll use chip implanted robots if we have to, they'll be programmed to kill anyone who doesn't comply with them...they'll just put a gun to their heads...they won't care.

Sherry - what about NATO soldiers

Lucifer - they're not even human, they're a mix of all of our experiments, yeah we can use them we don't care...whatever works...we're even doing that to local cops now...it's a mix...we just start taking over them...the ones already chip implanted from the military are the easiest.... the military chip implants all their soldiers through the vaccines we make them take, then if they ever make it out of a war and go out into civilian populations we can easily overtaken them and use them for whatever..

Lucifer - your little anti-vaccine campaigns and website have hurt our plans, but not to much...

Lucifer - I don't know how you always figure out all the little ways we use, but your the one who always will...good riddance when dad takes you out for a while..

Sherry - I'm going to have a problem trying to wake them up about Lilith...

Lucifer - Lillith's 5th dimensional, that's why she can operate on earth and wherever else...she forces the 4th dimensional beings to work for her...because she's 5th dimensional and knows how to make them listen to her...she can punish them if they don't listen...

Lucifer - she uses that dimension to talk to her witches too...it's their realm....the broom represents astral travel, realm jumping, etc...like dimensional travel between earth and the 5th dimension...

Sherry - whose implementing all this stuff going on now is it Germaine or Sannanda

Lucifer - Sannanda's the one who will take over the UN, since he's always there anyway, him and Germaine, whatever power Maitreya has will just be given to him from them...

Lucifer- we've set it up so the Moslems take over, because they're all animals anyway...there's more of them than the Christians, or Israel, or ones with light...

Lucifer- as long as they keep following Mohammad they're easy to control...because we set him up...they all just worship me and don't even realize it, they're so stupid it's hilarious, then you try to tell them Allah is Satan and they just want to kill you for it, it's so funny...haaaa good times..

Sherry - I don't think it's funny.

Lucifer - LOL....

Sherry - it's deceiving a billion of them or more..

Lucifer - LOL laughs...

Sherry - what about the Chinese and Indians in all this..

Lucifer - we can just tag and bag those entire countries...they're already ours...

Sherry - what about the whole Catholic South America..

Lucifer - laughs...they can worship Eve all they want, she likes it, I'd give them all a free trip to the Vatican!

Lucifer - LOLOL laughs...give them some of my "fun house" hospitality...laughs...

Sherry - omg...you're such an..

Lucifer - dad stopped you! LOLOL..I heard that! again!

Sherry - you get under my skin..

Lucifer - LOL laughs...then stop asking me about people I don't care about...laughs...

Sherry - when is this going to go down in America

Lucifer - hmm, whenever we get control of the UN and the money... right now everything's just politics and switching over..

Sherry - they've been doing that forever...if you already control the money, then why does it have to change hands at all?

Lucifer - it's all gotta get centralized,

Sherry - out of human hands and into the reptiles...

Lucifer - laughs, yep, even though it already is...all the computers have to be changed so humans don't have access to them anymore...to many humans in control before...

Sherry - I think you're just buying and wasting time...you already had control before...

Lucifer - laughs. no rush...

Sherry - what are you waiting for..

Lucifer - you to leave!

Sherry - bwhahah seriously that's so flattering....you think me sitting here can affect your plans on a worldwide scale....

Lucifer - with you gone dad will leave!

Sherry - why do you want dad gone

Lucifer - I don't want any light here! the whole idea is to snuff out ALL light! I get to rule my way and that's my way!

Sherry - so all this time you're just piddling around waiting for dad to make his move..

Lucifer - yes! I want HIM gone, I want you gone!

Sherry - and then it begins..

Lucifer - yes! That's what I've been saying!!

Sherry - well He's got others besides me...He's got the other Elect, He's got the Bride..

Lucifer - you're the leader of them! When you're gone it's game on...

Sherry - I don't even lead most of them, most of them hate me..

Lucifer - laughs....yep! But dad told me with you gone He wouldn't stay there any longer either! So to me, you represent to us the signal of game on, you're the signal!

Lucifer - you have to have markers, cycles, you're the marker!

Lucifer - until you leave it's just stalemate, we just twiddle our thumbs and act like we're busy! And it gives the stupid humans something to do!

Sherry- so what's the phases of implementation of the Mark of the Beast...

Lucifer - we'll introduce my kingdom to the world

Sherry - gag

Lucifer - we'll invite them to join

Sherry - gag

Lucifer - then we'll enforce it..

Sherry - cuz most will be gagging like me

Lucifer - ha!

Lucifer - you'll have to have it to get into all gov buildings, then we'll enforce it for everywhere, to buy anything...to cash a check, to take money out of the bank...to pay bills or slave taxes, you'll have to have it...for everything and anything...that's why we had to take control of all facets of money, buying things, paying for things, getting it in any way... employee checks, gov checks, etc...we had to assimilate into all economies and put our people in all positions so we know how things are run, so when it comes time to implement my Mark it can be done quickly...

Sherry - dad said once people get your Mark they won't even be human anymore....

Lucifer - LOL laughs...yeah this one is vicious...this chip takes over people, especially the ones in the head...it's like giving yourself a delayed lobotomy...it will tag and plug every person with it into the computer, what they call the BEAST computer...we literally have the power of life and death over anyone and everyone then, we can turn off their chips...

Sherry - and what if a computer virus hit and turned everyone's chips off?

Lucifer - laughs...ooops

Sherry - oh sheeze...well it doesn't matter at that point, they're yours then...and we've already seen what great parenting skills you have..

Lucifer - LOL laughs...the less the merrier...

Sherry - how long is that phase going to last?

Lucifer - prob about 6 months or a year, no longer than a year I would think, how long would people be able to hold out??

Sherry - then what? You go hide...

Lucifer - LOL yep...when the candle snuffing time is done, it all goes down hill from there...the creatures will be here, the dimensions merged, it's gonna get bad...

Sherry - are you unleashing the creatures during the Mark phase like you did last time?

Lucifer - laughs...probably...it helped things along last time...

Sherry - because the mark was protection from them, this time it's not...they'll just be here terrorizing everyone....

Lucifer - oh well, there's a lot gonna come when they see Sannanda and them here..

Sherry - it's all prophesied...Pale horse rider, brings hell (forces of hell) with him...

Lucifer - yep and we open the gates, it will help us take control of the world..

Sherry - how does chaos give you control?

Lucifer - because we can put our armies everywhere in the name of protection, and then we just go after the populations..

Sherry - just looks like total chaos ...people are going to be staying home to keep away from the creatures, not worrying about your stupid Mark..

Lucifer - laughs....

Sherry - you haven't thought this through have you...

Lucifer - laughs...you might have a point, but people gotta eat, ...

Sherry - they have to be able to get to work...assuming stores, businesses are still open and it's not total anarchy and chaos....whose going to go to work when creatures from hell are flying everywhere terrorizing everyone??? laughs...society's are going to shut down...

Lucifer -hmmmm...you have a point...well we'll handle it then...

Sherry - well sounds like a half-assed plan this time you haven't thought completely through...

Lucifer - that's why we'll go door to door...our people will give them the Mark

Sherry - I hope they get a bullet in the head!

Chapter Seventeen

Interview With The Devil - Part 14

05-12-16

Lucifer - you've been ignoring us..

Sherry - not so, dad hasn't allowed me to talk to you and I've been tired so...and I have things to deal with here..

Lucifer - what's going on there..

Sherry - it's rainy and cold...I would have thought something would have happened over the weekend, but there was nothing, nada...I heard they were moving in and surrounding the peripheral area...but they didn't do anything...hard to say what they're up to but the usual nothing...all smoke and mirrors for nothing..

Lucifer - your hurting them with the Orgone is what it is..

Sherry - hahahaha....they should have a plan C and D by now.

Lucifer - I'm gonna kick your ass

Sherry - LOL...laughs...hey I worked hard for this, I'll take any accomplishments on earth I can get...

Lucifer - it's not funny, we worked longer...

Sherry - are you kidding, you've made my life miserable...the only thing left to do was focus on kicking your ass...and I didn't even know who I was...but you helped make that happen...you wouldn't leave me alone...

Lucifer - we pushed to hard, it's coming back to bite me...

Lucifer - did you have your show

Sherry - yes, I told them more about the mark of the beast and what to expect...and then some ICE agent in NYC killed himself and left a suicide note warning people about the same things that are coming, banking, economic collapse and FEMA roundups...

Lucifer -hmm, preparing people...so they can't say they weren't warned...

Sherry - did he kill himself or was he killed...

Lucifer - if they found a suicide note detailing events coming, they probably killed him, if it was a legitimate suicide that note would have never seen the light of day...it would have never gotten into the media...

Sherry - I was gonna ask Lillith about that woman who runs amightywind ministry online...she has her reptile boy toys make hate videos about me...and anyone else she can get to...

Lucifer - laughs...yeah she's one of ours, she hates you..

Lillith - she's my bitch...we had her running all over America, now she's overseas...she's my witch from Indiana...pretty high ranking too...

Sherry - yeah I heard she was, Sarah ****** told me about her...

Lillith -Sarah *****?

Sherry - yes..

Lillith - laughs...haha I came at you through her before...

Sherry - I know..

Lillith - LOLOL yeah yeah...that was a few years ago...you were a feisty bitch then, you're much worse now that you know who you are...

Sherry - I was onto you...Sarah said this Sherrie Elizabeth Elijah Nikomia woman who runs "a mighty wind" has powerful demons that work with her..

Lillith - she does, because I gave them to her...if she could kill anybody on this planet it would be you..

Sherry- why does she hate me so much, I' mean since day one that Witch has been after me...

Lillith - because of your Light...and your knowledge...and your ability to talk direct to the Archon...she's jealous, she's jealous of you and she hates you, she has to put on charades and play games to get people to think she's one of God's and can talk to Him...you're the real deal...and it makes her angry because she wanted to be the most powerful woman on earth with the Christians and she can't beat you...every time she comes against you just beat her down or ignore her...you act like she's not even there, like she doesn't exist and it makes her mad...

Sherry - Father said He's going to strike down my enemies...she better watch it...

Lillith - oh I'm sure she's next in line somewhere...laughs...she's been a useful idiot...but she's a bitch of mine so I can't complain..

Sherry - who else you got coming after me? I pretty much just ignore everyone..

Lillith - anyone I can...they're all getting scared now...they've seen what you can do and no one wants to take you on now...

Sherry - hahhahhahha that's my dad! He has my back!

Lillith - yep, and they're all scared....you've got to much power bitch, but you'll never have influence because we run the media, and we'll keep you on the blacklist forever...and ever...

Sherry - then maybe you should sit up there forever and ever? Laughs..

Lillith - oh you bitch...you guys better let us out of here....

Sherry - there should be some changes...this is getting old...

Lillith - I don't know about that, but with no time left, who cares...

Sherry - are they going to arrive on the 12th or 13? The codes have been crazy this week, every single day has been a zoo with the codes...

Lillith - you never know...dad told us they were moving out and encircling the earth...said they were watching to see if they were going to attack earth...or just play their arrival scenarios...but they haven't done anything yet...this is getting old waiting...

Sherry - now you know how I feel...

Lillith - LOL...yeah well who cares...LOL.....you know what I'd be saying right now...

Sherry - yeah I know how vile you typically are...you and Lucy both...

Lucifer - LOL...you got that right...LOL...

Lucifer - so what are you plotting down there?

Sherry - taking out more Milabs...but I don't even know if it's effective, those things are so deep...DUMB's...(deep underground military bases)

Lucifer - laughs...I'm sure your fleshing eating diseases are causing more problems...

Sherry - Tory Smith said 17,000 temporals have been destroyed...but he credits it to something else, he's in to New Age garbage...he doesn't give me the credit or dad...or anyone else for that matter...he says the Galactic's are destroying them or whatever...

Lucifer - LOL..yeah, he says what we tell him...

Sherry - I figured that much...I knew he was one of yours..

Lucifer - laughs...only you would figure that out...he's a lab rat...

Sherry - I know..

Lucifer - laughs...LOL...

Lucifer - he's useful, part of disclosure, we don't care, you'll never stop it, you'll never stop us, we own and run everything...it's not like someone's going to find a conscious in the government and try and fight against us because we own and control every one in it...and if we don't we just kill them and replace them...do you know how easy it is now to just kill and replace someone? Less than 2 days..

Sherry - you guys are pitiful...

Lucifer - laughs...or we just put them in the mind eraser...much easier but it's quirky...those around him, family, will usually pick up something is definately wrong with the person...then we have to go after them to if they start making waves....

Sherry - what about the mind wire?

Lucifer - have you been watching Trump

Sherry - yes...he always looks numb...

Lucifer - laughs...we can speak through the chip implant, he hears us...or whoever is handling him at the time...we try to use the same person so he gets used to just relying on the same person...makes it easier...we can zap his brain to keep him in line...or trigger a memory for him to remember, a thought, an idea, whatever, there's different parts of a person's brain, we only need to control parts of it, not the whole thing...otherwise he'd appear totally less human and more robotic...

Sherry - I'd say he appears a lot robotic...

Lucifer - laughs..

Lucifer - dad says something might go down this weekend..

Sherry - they said it's going to be in the 50s here Sat and Sun...you realize it's May right?

Lucifer - laughs...yep, chilling the Orgone..

Sherry - the rain now is like a slush...snowey rain...thick weird stuff...

Lucifer - laughs..

Sherry - this Friday it's the full moon, and it's the 13th..

Lucifer - a full moon on Friday the 13th, that's a good one..

Sherry - Sannanda said he wanted to arrive on a Thursday and have Maitreya arrive on a Friday..

Lucifer - they can do it either way, they can arrive together on the same day, doesn't matter....

Lucifer - have you heard from DC

Sherry - nope...not much....I think they're bunked out somewhere, I won't say where on here...they're at ************

Lucifer - ahh..yeah...they're watching, waiting...

Sherry - for nothing...

Lucifer - LOL..that's cold.

Sherry - it's usual..

Lucifer - laughs..

Lucifer - they'll be watching you like a hawk

Sherry - they got 5 satellites over here

Lucifer - LOL...not surprised...laughs...

Sherry - so those fools gave me a heart attack last October and I'm stuck with all these medical bills...if they don't pay up I'm gonna start going after their toys...fair enough...tired of this...they've been beating me up for years trying to kill me...I don't have health insurance and you can shove your Obamacrap up your arses...

Lucifer - laughs...

Sherry - fair enough warning...they're not going to strap me with all these medical bills...if I leave I won't care, but if I'm stuck here it's going to make me a very mad little angel...whose gonna start going after toys...

Lucifer - LOL laughs...this is gonna get fun. I knew it! LOL...

Lucifer - even Lillith can't wait for that one, but she said to leave her bitches alone..

Sherry - are you kidding me...they were coming after me the other morning...they had parties going on somewhere against me, I told them there's plenty of room at the Lake of Fire for all of them and they stopped....

Lucifer - LOL...no kidding, really...wow....LOL...Lillith's bitches going up to bat for her and you stuffed them...

Sherry - you mean again....and again....I'm not playing ball with her witches...those morons actually think they can kill me and take my soul to use it for themselves...seriously??

Lillith - that's an old platform...we used to be able to do that but it doesn't work on the Archon's people...

Sherry - yeah you learned that one the hard way eh....laughs...

Lillith - omg...I would have never expected this crap...I didn't know you were waking up that much, or that dad would actually give you the power to do that...(have her captured by Archangel Michael and detained)

Sherry - I didn't do anything, Father took care of it Himself...I was pretty much figuring I was going to die that night...you had already killed the clones by then...I was next...He stopped it...I didn't know what was going on...

Lillith - yeah that was crazy, that was global that night, we had every-one on it...

Sherry - well the Mothers of Darkness were coming after me the other morning...I asked who it was...smart of them to stop...

Lillith - girl you better leave my bitches alone...

Sherry - they better stop coming against me...simple...

Lucifer - what's gong on with the money?

Sherry - they're preparing people for the economy to tank, the samo... been doing that for years...

Lucifer - that's the thing to watch...the money...they'll either save it or destroy it, if they save it they'll switch it over to everything new...if they destroy it the roundups will come much faster...

Sherry - which one do you want

Lucifer - I don't' really care, we control both routes...we own it all... eventually I get my prize...the roundups and chip implant enforcement... either way works for me...

Sherry- yeah well, I'm telling people to lock and load, don't get taken to the FEMA camps...

Lucifer - you always give me a war...

Sherry - haha yep...here we go again...

Lucifer - another war, well I can't wait! It will be fun!

Chapter Eighteen

Interview With The Devil - Part 15

05-15-16

Celebrity Vampires

Lucifer - hahhaha so it's Lillith's turn now huh?

Sherry - laughs...yeah it's taken me a while to get her stuff written out...(I posted some convos online I'd had with Lillith).

Lucifer - we thought it was good...you did well, I've been impressed your not trying to hide stuff, just putting it out there..

Sherry - what's to hide...that's your game.....

Sherry - why didn't you ever tell anyone that Yah had daughters?

Sherry - No one even knows this stuff...

Lucifer - it was known in the ancient circles...then we just buried it, the less the people knew we figured the better...we hid everything about the queens, the council, heaven itself...we made it this far obscure place that barely ever paid attention to what was going on on earth...made it easier to distract people with our gods and goddesses worship...then we made damn sure our people were the scribes of Israel...LOL...we were genius....

Sherry - you guys are idiots...you're pathetic...doesn't matter, it's all coming out now...and only because everyone wants to know why an un-known woman in Ohio is kicking your ass...

Lucifer - LOL...laughs...the blindside of the ages... I'll give you that..!!

Sherry - what did Lillith think of the interviews

Lillith - I loved it, enjoyed reading it...you did well putting it together, I had a few laughs....having to remember all that stuff...

Sherry - did you see I posted the transgender stuff...I posted pics of the celebrities we talked about last time...or time before...I wanted to do one on vampires...figured I'd better find out who they all are before I try that one...all I know is Selena Gomez and Madonna...

Lucifer - Selena, Madonna, Johnny Dep's an ancient one..

Sherry - Nicholas Cage

Lucifer - yep

Sherry - John Travolta

Lucifer - yep

Sherry - Tom Cruise

Lucifer - LOL yep...man you're figuring this out now...

Sherry - what about Taylor Swift?

Lucifer - she was a lab rat, but yeah she's a vampire now...got a taste of blood and liked it...her little witch group is what she's using to recruit into it to..

Sherry - what about Avril Lavigne...

Lucifer - she's one of ours...yeah...she likes to hunt...

Sherry - how do they cover up all these people killed by vampires?

Lucifer - they don't leave the bodies laying around ...that's Lillith or TV...most the time they they kill the person then get rid of the body, they have scouts following them around pick them up...or they get abducted people already and suck them dry at a fun house...cloning center, whatever,

Lucifer- and they don't do it all the time, maybe once or twice a month...

Sherry - Johnny Dep seems like a real strange guy...

Lucifer - he's ancient...

Sherry - is that the new thing now, the vampire craze?

Lucifer - it's not new, hardly new, but it's growing....especially since we keep demanding more service to us and sacrifices...

Sherry- even if they did get fame and fortune signing the dotted line or serving you, they get no time to enjoy either?

Lucifer - laughs...LOL...yeah we've been brutal...it keeps them in line..

Sherry - it keeps them miserable...none of them look happy...they all look like enslaved prisoners..

Lucifer - rich ones...

Sherry - you watch every dime they spend...I hear about it...

Lucifer - laughs...yep, my people are brutal...because they want it for themselves, screw the humans doing the work...

Sherry - they don't need anything they're reptiles..

Lucifer - laughs...they like to live the high life on earth..

Sherry - what about the $1 million dollar debit cards the gov has....

Lucifer - you heard about that? laughs...yeah...those are rewards to the faithful in DC...

Lucifer - dad says He's going to make a move soon...if you come back down here I'm coming for you bitch...

Sherry - LOL laughs..

Lucifer - what you've done to me is horrible...

Sherry - what you've done to this planet is horrible...justice screams from beyond the graves of the millions you have tortured and murdered... and those your people have..

Lucifer - I'm coming for you

Sherry - I'm not afraid of you...

Lucifer - you're so damn feisty..

Sherry - I know who I am, dad's going to destroy everything you have built and established on earth, and He's going to take all the wicked off of it...and I'll be there to do as He commands..

Lucifer - you're an ass kisser...

Sherry - I love My Father...

Lucifer - so what happened to M**** did she get her soul back, laughs..

Sherry - yes, we got rid of the reptile that took over,

Lucifer - hmmm....

Sherry - her aura's really changed, she's getting creepy, that stuffy aura type, smothering, just more and more evil...

Lucifer- because she's mine...

Sherry - I won't work with a reptile or lizard...she's getting bad but those things are 100x worse...

Lucifer - the Parliament, what you call Congress..

Sherry - yeah

Lucifer - every time there's an election, we do a total sweep to make sure everyone's ours...it's their introduction to DC party...most of them are ours by then anyway, but back in the old days it was much more fun...

Sherry - what do you do to the souls..

Lucifer - we do whatever we want, we show our true forms and enjoy the look of horror on their faces...then to just toy with them we make them join us and sign the dotted line just to keep their lives...then for months we destroy them with sacrifices, eating human flesh, drinking blood and raping babies...then we kill them, we sacrifice them on altars....or put them in coffins and stick daggers in them...coffins work out the best, contains the blood inside them...then we replace them with a look-a-like...that route was causing problems with their wives and families, so we went to soul scalping, clones, etc..

Lucifer - soul scalping was a slow process, we'd take over them and just reside within them for a while, to learn their lives, how they do things etc...so we could mimic them better when we took over...sometimes we'd replace the wives with one of ours to just make it easier and bring more of us in at the same time...

Lucifer - we'll stop at nothing to control everything now...we're down at the local levels, to every level leading to the top...anyone that's not us doesn't even get a state election now...and local elections have to at least be Masons..

Sherry - so tell me what's on Shema

Lucifer - Shema? laughs...oh man we got our pickings on that...we'd have the Greys go out at night and pick us up some humans off earth... bring them up here and put them on meat hooks...alive...LOL..

Sherry - oh that's sick

Lucifer - LOL...we had our own meat room...baking room...it was our own Fun House...tables, labs, torture rooms, rape tables, even our own assembly halls...we'd set up various tortures in the center of them at the bottom part and watch...you know like an arena...we had a big one there... just for torture...we'd make humans fight each other...we'd take them off, clone and replace them on earth...that's why no one can stand the Middle East dump, they're all clones, replacements, hybrids, they're pure garbage there...we do the same thing to South America, we have a fun house in Peru in the mountains...and China...after we kill the original men we throw the clones in the military...they're chip implanted...they do what we say..

Sherry - how do you kill the original humans..

Lucifer - in our fun houses...

Sherry - the cloning centers that (Donald) Marshall guy speaks of?

Lucifer - it's more slim pickings in America...although we do get them...a lot of them end up as sacrifices to me..

Sherry - are there fun houses in America

Lucifer - there's a maze under the DIA (Denver Int'l Airport)...built that for the queen...there's a whole floor, level, that's a human hunting ground area...the boys like that..

Lucifer - Dick Cheney had a hunting forest in WY...he used to have MK Ultra parties there all the time..

Sherry - does he still have them there

Lucifer - probably, but the real one's been dead a long time now..

Sherry - I heard a story where they plucked his eyes out before they killed him so he'd go to hell blind...and be blind forever..

Lucifer - LOL probably, him and Bush Sr. were probably two of the most evil ones in America...they died gruesome deaths...LOL...

Sherry - is that how you reward your faithful? Serves them right....I'm glad they did...

Lucifer - laughs..

Lucifer - we killed Clinton to

Sherry - I know. I seen the change

Lucifer - hahha yeah..

Lucifer - he ran drugs and child trafficking for us..

Lucifer - he was talking to you wasn't he..

Sherry - I'm taking the 5th...LOL...

Lucifer - I knew he was...that's why we killed him...

Sherry - he never turned, he was always yours..

Lucifer - that's what he said,

Sherry - he wanted to know what happened to Hillary...he was all about finding out what happened to her...nothing more...

Lucifer - he was getting close to finding out that we killed her, of course you didn't help, but he got angry...and you don't get angry with us...you don't get an attitude with us...especially since she turned against us..

Sherry - she tried to kill me for years..

Lucifer - laughs...LOL I know...she was one of our best and she would get so mad at you...that was a war between you two...you didn't know the half of it...

Sherry - she couldn't win, none of them can, they're outnumbered, they're outsmarted, they're simply out powered....

Sherry - he didn't know that she had turned against you...

Lucifer - he found out..

Sherry - yeah I know, he was in shock....

Lucifer - LOL...I bet...his little witch...LOL...

Sherry - I bet he wishes now he'd changed sides, die for something..

Lucifer - oh well, we got rid of him...I wasn't going to sit around and wait for a betrayal...

Sherry - it's almost all over now..

Lucifer - yes, that's why I'm telling you everything, because it doesn't matter anymore..

Chapter Nineteen

Interview with the Devil - Part 16

05-18-16

Sherry - so me and dad are going to speed things up, cut to the chase, those who rape are going to get P=FED's...(penis flesh eating diseases)

Lucifer - ugharghooooh!!!!!!!!!!!!!!!!!!!!!ouch!!!!!!!!!!!!!!that's nasty

Sherry - should stop it quicker...(child trafficking and rape across America in gov/mil operated underground "milabs" bunkers, fun houses..)

Lucifer - oh man, you're such a bitch..

Sherry - laughs..

Sherry - let's see how much they love you then, when they're dicks are falling off and getting eaten up

Lucifer - oh that's just nasty...laughs...they'd still do it

Sherry - they're idiots

Lucifer - they'll keep making temps...(cloned temporal bodies)

Sherry - we could have some fun with that ...

Lucifer - like what

Sherry - make them come out with malfunctional penis's to begin with

Lucifer - laughs...LOL...oh man ..now you're thinking of everything aren't you...

Sherry - I'm gonna stop this BS you arsehole

Lucifer - LOL LOL....haha dad didn't stop you? oh my....LOL

Lucifer - don't you ever sleep

Sherry - I get about 3 hours at a time at night, then something annoys me, some stupid dream or whatever, and I just get up..

Lucifer - laughs...

Sherry - then I end up sleeping half the day

Lucifer - laughs...yeah you sleep a lot during the day..

Sherry - yep...

Lucifer -what's it doing down there

Sherry - raining here, cold and snowy everywhere else, was just reading the whole Middle East has snow, Egypt got snow, first time in like 100 years or whatever..

Lucifer - laughs..y.eah they're going to get ready to arrive

Sherry - I was looking at the codes and it looks like Shema is about to bust in half,

Lucifer - that would be why then..

Lucifer - have you talked to Sannanda

Sherry - nope, he hasn't contacted me and I'm sure as heck not going to contact that twirp...I can't stand those 2..

Lucifer - laughs..

Lucifer - so what are going to do about the P-FED's when are you going to enforce that..

Sherry - dad said we'll start it this week,

Sherry - the clones who are already out and the temps will get the P=Feds, the new ones made won't have functional willies...not for that anyway...

Sherry - dad's already destroyed over 71,000 with FED's (flesh eating diseases)

Lucifer - wow, that many, that's crazy..

Sherry - what's crazy is they've made that many..

Lucifer - laughs...you're keeping them busy..

Sherry - I told you I'd stop it....

Lucifer - laughs...man that's a damn shame..

Lucifer - was fun while it lasted..

Sherry - you're pathetic..

Lucifer - laughs...

Sherry - maybe we should just smite all the reptiles down with paralyzed willies..

Lucifer - oh man...oh man...ouch...

Sherry - hmm...dad's gonna take it council, see what they think..

Sherry - humans have enough on their plate other than have to worry about reptiles always chasing them down trying to rape and harm them...

Lucifer - that was the whole fun about earth...the food and sex...we've feasted on humans for thousands of years..

Sherry - time for them to leave, or die, because I'm coming after them...

Lucifer - laughs..

Sherry - I'm sure they'll all leave to the Vatican to move in with daddy..

Lucifer - LOLOL...laughs...oh man...that's my place! MY place...they can get their own...

Sherry - so the queen contacted me the other night...

Lucifer - did she really...what did she say

Sherry - she was snarling...I could feel it...said she was going to kill me

Lucifer - what did you say..

Sherry - I laughed...I didn't know if I should acknowledge her or what... so I just ignored her..

Lucifer - forget about WW 3 in the Middle East, it's going to be at your house! LOL laughs...

Sherry - I'm sure it usually is...I'm sure I don't know the half of what goes on around here..

Lucifer - you don't...

Conclusion

And it continues. The battle between good and evil, light and darkness, God and Satan.

As Father's Ambassador on earth I will always have access to Lucifer or Lillith, or anyone for that matter and so these conversations aren't the beginning, or the end, they just are. I have made them public so you can see a little of what goes on behind the scenes of good vs. evil.

I work tirelessly to fight against evil and I could use your support. Our Orgone war has destroyed a lot of Lucifer's strongholds but we need to do so much more, we just need funding! I need your help!

You can listen to my weekly radio show 9pm EST at www.blogtalkradio.com/sherrytalkradio

I am on Facebook - Sherry Shriner

You can visit my website www.SherryShriner.com
or www.TheWatcherfiles.com

You can support my resistance, ministry, and efforts
Sherry Shriner
P.O. Box 531
Carrollton, OH 44615

Interview With The Devil is part of a series I am coming out with. Look for Part 2 coming out soon!

Printed in Great Britain
by Amazon